BOURNEMOUTH

CURIOSITIES

W.A. HOODLESS

The
History
Press

The world's largest deckchair
Weighing the same as an adult elephant and measuring 28ft tall and 33ft long, this giant deckchair appeared on Bournemouth beach in March 2012. It was commissioned by the drinks brand, Pimms, was removed, and then returned as a permanent display in August 2012 following petitions. 'Deckchairs are so quintessentially British, they affect our personality' (sculptor Stuart Murdoch). (Photograph by W.A. Hoodless)

First published 2012

The History Press
The Mill, Brimscombe Port
Stroud, Gloucestershire, GL5 2QG
www.thehistorypress.co.uk

British Library Cataloguing in Publication Data.
A catalogue record for this book is available from the British Library.

ISBN 978 0 7524 6459 6

Typesetting and origination by The History Press
Printed and bound in Great Britain by
Marston Book Services Limited, Didcot

Contents

	Introduction	5
1.	Seaside Humour and the BIC Sculpture	7
2.	Southbourne Fights the Sea	10
3.	From the Devil to Laurel and Hardy	14
4.	Oldest House Imponderable	19
5.	Labrador, Police and Pond	22
6.	Tregonwell and his Great Accidental Invention	24
7.	Bard of Bournemouth	31
8.	Pine Trees – The Great Enablers	37
9.	Bourne Takes a Joke in 1816	44
10.	Shopwalkers, Package Transport and Father Christmas	49
11.	Of Lightning and Ashes	52
12.	The Queen's Ancestor and Stourfield House	55
13.	Satire on the Sands	61
14.	A Ukrainian and Two Kings on the Beach	63
15.	Albany	68
16.	Longest Fireman's Pole	73
17.	Mayor Whitelegg and Some Recollections	76
18.	Faltering Start but a High-Speed Finish	79
19.	Remedies at a Watering Place	85
20.	Of Plank, Smuggling-Outrage and Chapel	88
21.	Astonishing Drainage System	91
22.	Undercliff Drive Monster	97
23.	Smuggling at Fisherman's Walk	101
24.	Growing Pains	102
25.	World Record for One Day	106
26.	Strange Case of the Beales Fire	109
27.	Ensbury Manor, Smuggling and Ghosts	112
28.	Eleven Quirks in Brief	116
	Bibliography	123
	Index	125

Introduction

The purpose of this book is to provide a whole batch of curious stories – no easy task, because so much has already been written about the town. Yet it is extraordinary how fresh research will reveal new angles or 'extras'.

The chapters fall into one of two categories. In the first place are some curiosities that are so little-known that they must generally be new to the reader. Secondly, we have chapters dealing with known material but revealing surprising features, which throw fresh light on the subject. Indeed, a number of stories have been purposely excluded where there are no significant 'extras'. Sometimes, the new items are not directly connected with the chapter's subject but can hopefully be regarded as indirect yet intriguing snippets. There is even the occasional illustration not referred to in the text. Definition is always an issue for books dealing with curious things – where do you draw the line between local interest and the curious? The reader's indulgence may be necessary for this grey area. Hence, there is no attempt here to provide the usual Bournemouth history. Rather, the idea is to add some curiosities to the known world of local interest in a random fashion, with the context sometimes taking us away from the town. Since Bournemouth's curiosities vary from the serious to the humorous, with all shades in between, my hope is that the reader will be as fascinated as I have been to delve into the whys and wherefores of some big issues and the quirky nature of the small ones.

I am very grateful to a number of people who have been most helpful. In no particular order, they are: Nigel Beale; Mrs Julia Smith; Sir Mervyn Medlycott; Sir George Meyrick; Ian Stevenson; Ted Baker; Joan Harrington; Peter Gayler from Albany; Shaun Richardson from St Peter's Church; John Butterworth of the Chine Hotel; the O2 Academy; J.P. Morgan; Kim Hall of Wessex Water; Jenny Briancourt, Matilda Richards and their colleagues at The History Press; Paul Ambrose, David Harlow, Stuart Clarke and Nick Colledge of Bournemouth Council; Michael Doland; Rod Haskell; Derek Wareham, ex-fire brigade; Jonathan Sells, sculptor; Mark Greenhow of the Laurel & Hardy Museum; Philip Whitelegg, ex-Mayor; Mr Richards regarding Kinson Manor Farmhouse; Paul Lawton of the Royal Exeter Hotel; Steve Cox of Treecall Consulting; Michael Stead, particularly for his maps of the early town; Peter Kazmierczak and staff of the Heritage Zone at Bournemouth Central Library; and Jon Dunne concerning the Shelley Theatre.

Inevitably, the required research had to range far and wide, including the internet. Sometimes, it was possible to verify facts from original sources or check them in some other fashion. However, where this could not be done, the item is described as 'estimated' or 'reported', etc. Any errors that remain must be my own responsibility. Where material is still in copyright and it has been possible to establish that, I have the permission of the owners to reproduce it. I would, however, apologise for any accidental offence that may have been caused in cases where I have been unable to trace the owner.

W.A. Hoodless, 2012

The Bournemouth Eye
Situated in the Lower Gardens, the giant helium balloon (surface area 0.38 acres) is Bournemouth's highest attraction, offering passengers a panoramic view across the town between March and October from 500ft up in the air. (Courtesy of Matilda Richards)

ONE

Seaside Humour and the BIC Sculpture

*I*t was felt that the Bournemouth International Centre (opened in September 1984 and known as the BIC) needed a suitable sculpture in recognition of the town's enormous progress since its foundation. Rather strangely, some fifteen years elapsed before the sculpture was commissioned and provided, but no matter – better late than never! Portland stone was used to depict two main players from the history of Bournemouth: Lewis Tregonwell, the recognised town founder, and Christopher Crabbe Creeke, architect and surveyor, who later facilitated its fast advancement with roads, buildings and drainage schemes. Both men were highly influential in the town's development.

The unusual 7ft 6in-high sculpture (Figs 1-3) is situated close to the pavement in front of the BIC. There is an obvious question – what exactly was the thinking behind it? Well, that all depends upon who is giving the reply. Views range from an 'expression of civic pride' to a 'quirky depiction of key figures from history'. Yet whatever were the intentions of the original brief to the artist, such matters are not completely fixed in advance – much rightly depends on the sculptor's creativity and interpretation. Despite an initial meeting of councillors at the BIC to consider and approve a small clay model of the proposed work, some changes were to be expected.

Professional sculptor Jonathan Sells, of Corfe Castle, has kindly provided the rather strange background. Tregonwell is the person given credit for founding Bournemouth in 1810, as celebrated in 1910 and 2010. He bought land that year and built a house first occupied in 1812, a house now incorporated into the Royal Exeter Hotel. The new summer residence was really for his wife Henrietta, who was still grieving over the sad death of their son in infancy. He went on to acquire more land, build several properties and create the tiny village of Bourne Tregonwell. Once the early town was established, the new Commissioners, under the Bournemouth Improvement Act of 1856, needed someone like Creeke to take it forward very swiftly. Whilst this may explain the sculptor's brief, decisions were still required, i.e. just how were these two figures to be shown?

Perhaps the most controversial part is the WC on which Creeke is perched. The pan is discreetly placed, facing away from the road and hardly visible to the casual observer in Exeter Road. The reason for it is simply the work behind his job title: Inspector of Nuisances. The harsh fact is that someone had to plan the drainage upgrades for the new fashionable watering place known as Bournemouth, because large numbers of cesspools and septic tanks were not quite the thing. Creeke is pensively stroking his very large beard and actually pointing sadly behind him to the rich and renowned founder. Is he wondering just why he is less appreciated? Was his sterling town development work not enough? Although there is a Wetherspoons public house named after him in Holdenhurst Road, even now he gets less recognition.

But there is more to the story of how the WC pan came to be included. The first idea was to place Creeke on Bournemouth Pier, and a flat area began to be carved out of the stone. That area can still just be seen in the finished sculpture. However, once Jonathan discovered more about Creeke's drainage role in the early town, he could not resist suggesting the idea of the pan. The response was, 'Why not?'

Before visiting Bourne Chine with his wife, Tregonwell was already familiar with it from his time as a captain in the Dorset Volunteer Rangers. He had two key responsibilities: to defend the coast against risk of invasion in Napoleonic times and to combat the smuggling trade. However, rumours persist today that he was really part of that extensive and profitable industry himself. If so, he would not have been the only ambivalent or hypocritical member of high society to be on both sides of the law. A close inspection of the sculpture will reveal two tubs of brandy and a smugglers' boat behind the Town Hall – a town having a respectable façade, yet with secrets round the back. However, we must not judge the industry too harshly from our armchairs, because for many poor people the choice was stark – join the smuggling trade or risk starving to death.

An even closer inspection, for which one has to climb the wall by the pavement, will also reveal the squirrels. They are near to the smugglers' boat and in their frequently observed state of fast running. Rightly or wrongly, the grey squirrel is unpopular with many in Bournemouth but, nevertheless, does still need to survive. They were included to demonstrate that need.

The founder is placed over the Town Hall in all its majesty, wearing a rather smug or self-satisfied expression. Yet a piece of crumpled paper is depicted (intentionally greatly out of scale) at the back door of the Town Hall. Does this imply a lack of propriety? It is hard to be sure, and Jonathan Sells will only say that it is a piece of 'waffle'! Certainly, the idea of the bucket and spade (held by Tregonwell behind his back) is to show that the founder is playing and having a good time – quite a contrast with the serious Creeke.

On a different note, the carving of Tregonwell shows him holding a scroll with the names of the three Bournemouth-born recipients of the Victoria Cross: Cpl C.R. Noble, Sgt F.C. Riggs and Lt-Col. D.A. Seagrim. There is, of course, nothing to be read into this feature except full and due respect for their extreme valour.

As might be expected, there was controversy. Although the Mayor, Keith Rawlings, liked the sculpture generally, and indeed had personally paid over £10,000 for it due to a certain lack of finance or commitment from the council, he did not like the squirrels. The *Telegraph* reported in May 1999 that several residents seemed less than pleased about the WC pan, but this was countered by the Mayor: 'It is a very witty interpretation of my request for a statue which celebrates the life of two very important figures in the history of the town.' Jonathan Sells regards it as a 'slice of seaside humour'. The *Echo* felt that it would be a dull old world if everything we looked at or experienced in our lives was governed by rules or regulations incapable of taking the existence of a sense of humour into the equation.

So it is, that in front of a prestigious international conference centre, some diverse and quirky aspects of a town's history are laid bare in a most attractive and skilful sculpture.

The bucket and spade tell a story
How very significant that Tregonwell has the fun of playing on the beach whilst Creeke is ruminating on the WC pan, doubtless planning his next drainage scheme. (Author's collection)

TWO

Southbourne Fights the Sea

*I*t is far from obvious that Bournemouth has had its historic battles with the sea. Nevertheless, the present 7 miles of fairly wide beach, the stable cliffs, and the protection of the roads and buildings at the top of the cliffs did not just happen. This chapter is a glimpse of one contest amongst many.

The town's justification for needing an effective coastal protection policy is the undesirable alternative of doing nothing. Left to itself, the sea can form a bay into a naturally sustainable shape through a system of destabilising soft cliffs by under-scouring and causing falls – a disaster for any roads and buildings on the cliff top. Assuming, therefore, that the sea creates a sustainable shape between fixed headlands and there is no sea-level rise, longshore sediment drift will be minimised and erosion reduced. However, protection will always be needed in Poole Bay because certain factors prevent such stability. These are that, although Old Harry is fixed, the other headland at Hengistbury is not fixed; that the tidal inlet to Poole Harbour complicates the drift; that the drift was never overwhelmed by sediment from cliff erosion before the sea walls were built; that no more cliff sediment is available due to these walls; that the walls reflect wave energy, thereby increasing the drift; and finally, that sea-level rise is also detrimental.

In the case of Southbourne's unprotected cliffs, the future was bleak in 1952 and a stand had to be taken. In pre-war days, development had definitely run ahead of coastal management. The sea was slowly but surely creating its preferred bay shape. Yet after 1932, a row of ten dwellings were erected on the sea side of the Southbourne Overcliff Drive, west of Southbourne Crossroads. From an aerial shot dated 1935, there were four bungalows at the eastern end, then five houses (including one under construction) and one house building plot. Only three should ever have been built – those at the eastern end of the row, on the site of Sandymount. Sandymount, a large house, had to be demolished before the three bungalows were erected, as it was too near to the eroding cliff face. However, it was possible to site the three new bungalows further away from the cliff than the other seven properties due to the curve of the road; these three are the only ones which survived.

Even earlier, in 1903, a sale plan was produced for the Southbourne-on-Sea Freehold Land Company Ltd. It showed Sandymount, which was then known as St Catherine's Home, about 130ft from the cliff edge. Just thirty years afterwards, the

Ordnance Survey shows the cliff edge about 40ft away from the building, implying a loss rate of 3ft per annum.

In January 1946, the *Echo* reported: 'At Solent Road, the cliff edge is only six feet from the garden wall of a house on the cliff drive. Most of the roadway has itself disappeared already.' This report is referring to the eastern part of the old Southbourne Cliff Drive, long since lost to erosion. There were several highly evocative house names, including Sea Spray, Wave Crest, Cliff Cottage, Spring Tide and Sea Foam. An extract from the 1933 OS map shows how much of the Drive had vanished by that date. It is evident that the eastern part of the Drive had been eroded first, with less than half the road width remaining in 1933. However, at the western part of the map extract, the full road, together with some level cliff beyond, was still there. In addition, the extract is marked with the 1964 cliff line, when the Drive had disappeared.

Properties eventually required rear access. Before the new Southbourne Coast Road, access for some was temporarily from Admiralty Road at the rear – at least the sea wall had been built, and the cliff graded and stabilised. A current photograph shows a property's rear garden boundary at the existing edge of the graded cliff. There used to be a normal road and further land between that garden boundary and the 1933 cliff edge. However, all is now well, due to the long-term success of the remedial works.

A picture was taken in February 1950 at the back of the houses by Crossroads. An August 1951 public enquiry heard that protection works were urgent. In March 1951, the occupier of the westernmost one had left his property for safety reasons, but

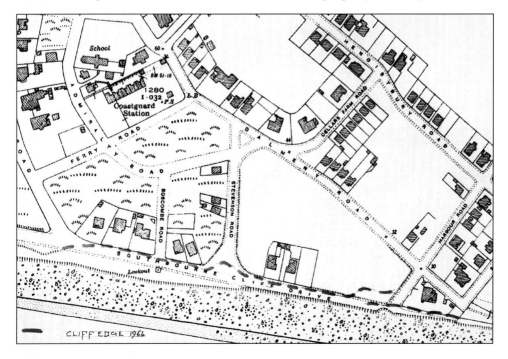

Cliff edge in 1964 at Southbourne
The 1933 stage of erosion is seen on the map by the partial loss of Southbourne Cliff Drive. The broken line shows the cliff edge in 1964 and 2012. (Ordnance Survey map 1933, © Crown copyright)

Graded cliff at Southbourne
A garden wall boundary is visible at the cliff top – it used to face on to the Cliff Drive, long since lost to erosion. (Author's collection)

he returned in June 1952 with considerable bravado. 'Of course, it's all been a lot of nonsense! My house was never in the slightest danger of falling. It's got the strongest foundations in Bournemouth, 11ft 6in of brick and concrete.'

Meanwhile, the essential work for the erosion barrier was in progress: two walls of steel piles at the cliff foot, three new groynes, and cliff-grading prior to cliff-planting for stability. In September 1952, the owner of a house three doors along noted a recent cliff fall and said that those in the middle were anxious about winter storms. There was 'no fear' at an eastern bungalow, but the 'far-west man' was less upbeat than in June, saying that 'the cliff should be built up more and the job was not nearly finished'. It must have been disconcerting for them, for as the *Bournemouth Times & Directory* stated on 2 September 1952: 'About 12 feet of cliff stands between the back doors of some of the houses and a 95-foot drop to the beach.'

By August 1956, the four worst affected houses were being sold to the council for demolition on grounds of safety. The westernmost house was virtually on the edge of the cliff by then and, if there was bravado, it went unreported. Instead, the owner remarked of his new house: 'I shall not be overlooking the sea I can tell you. I shall be right away from the gales.' At one time, some 36ft of his land had been lost in just three weeks. All four houses were being demolished in January 1957, after a life of around only twenty-two years. Although the cliff had been stabilised, it seems that it still needed to settle and it was unsafe to occupy them for any longer. The OS of 1975 shows that another three had been removed by that date, leaving just the three built on the Sandymount site.

House on cliff in 1950
A fence has fallen over the eroding edge behind a house which was sold to the council for demolition six years later.

Quite apart from the demolition of Sandymount and the problem of the 'row of ten', there were two other large houses that had to be demolished – Gorselands and Southbourne House (later hotel), shown on the 1933 map. In February 1957, the five-storey twenty-bedroom Southbourne House Hotel had seen a major cliff fall, which removed 6ft of lawn after heavy seas. In addition, soil cracks had appeared further back in the garden. Both buildings also obstructed the 1960s remedial engineering works, which included the new Southbourne Coast Road. The town's guide for 1938 advertised the Southbourne House Hotel as having perfect sea views – fair comment, as the site of its structure is now *south* of that new road. As for Gorselands, the block of flats erected on what was left of its site was named Cliff House.

In brief, the Southbourne engineering works of the 1950s and 1960s were an essential rescue operation which protected the buildings and roads for the future. The current cliff erosion rate of about 1cm a year is unaffected by the sea and is therefore limited to the impact of weather only. The fight was expensive but worth it.

THREE

From the Devil to Laurel and Hardy

he enormous Grand Theatre and Pavilion in Christchurch Road, which opened on 27 May 1895, has had a colourful history – a tribute to the farsightedness of that prolific Boscombe promoter, Councillor Archibald Beckett. However, even he could not have foreseen the part to be played by the Devil or Laurel and Hardy, still less the present occupiers O2 Academy.

After providing the large first-night party of corporation dignitaries with dinner at the nearby Salisbury Hotel (which he had also built), Beckett took them through the Arcade (which again he had built) into the side entrance of the theatre to the front stalls. However, the procession on foot of Deputy Mayor, Mace-Bearer, councillors, aldermen, Town Clerk and Borough Accountant had to run the gauntlet of the crowds and some good-humoured 'chaff'. They were dressed in scarlet robes and cocked hats, the hats being a subject of some controversy at the time and a likely cause of the chaff. After the National Anthem, a burlesque comic production of *Crusoe the Cruiser* was enjoyed by the estimated 2,000 to 3,000 attending. There were songs and dancing, an appreciated reference to the Balfour Case (the 1895 building society fraud), scenes including Crusoe's great-great-grandfather's hut at Margate Sands, a full chorus and ballet.

Apart from its use as an indoor circus for some of the time, the theatre provided drama for the first ten years. In those far-off days of competition with Bournemouth, the rapidly developing Boscombe was making sure it had its own pier, spa, arcade and theatre. A particular design feature was the grand organ keyboard that could swivel from the theatre to the Arcade, thereby entertaining shoppers by day and theatre-goers by night. Sir Henry Irving and Lillie Langtry were among the famous performers who graced the stage in those times of theatrical riches. Yet the playhouse was not quite realising its full potential. As for the circus, the lions were a slight problem. They used to be led from King's Park, where the enclosures were, underground through tunnels and into the boiler room of the theatre. Relocating them from their basement cages to the circus ring must have been interesting to say the least. Although members of the Bournemouth Civic Society actually saw the cages at the time of the 2007 upgrade to the building, there is nothing now visible as the access has been sealed. Fig.4 shows how some of the original features remain, despite the building's current use as a nightclub.

From 1905, when it was renamed the Boscombe Hippodrome and used as a music hall, there was greater success, including the likes of Marie Lloyd and Charlie Chaplin. Music and variety continued until its 1956 conversion to a dance venue – many will remember it as the Royal Ballrooms in the 1960s. More recently, it became Tiffany's and in 2008 the Opera House. Before opening as the Opera House, this listed building had undergone a huge £3.5 million refurbishment scheme, with a view to becoming a multi-use venue for the people of Boscombe. Now it is the O2 Academy nightclub.

In late Victorian times, many thought such places of entertainment lowered moral values. Indeed, there was an unsuccessful attempt to stop the construction job by landowners, clergy and the Temperance Movement. The builder opposite was also far from happy. Apparently, when he finished his building in 1896, a nude tableau was spotted advertising a forthcoming event. The theatre was hardly meeting Beckett's claim on the opening night (to cheers of 'Hear! Hear!' from his audience) that it 'would be his study to provide entertainments such as nobody could say a word against'. It was thus decided to shame the customers by fixing a statue of the Devil himself exactly opposite the main entrance to the theatre – it is still there. Equally, the objectors might have felt that all those entering the theatre would indeed be cursed by the Devil, which would serve them right!

Devil overlooks theatre at Boscombe
Placed up high and opposite the theatre's entrance, the inscription was: 'THE DEVIL COMES INTO HIS OWN.'
(Author's collection)

The inscription, which has long since been eroded away, read: 'THE DEVIL COMES INTO HIS OWN.' The builder's three-storey project is now five shops with flats above. The second-floor flats are set back several feet behind a terrace which runs above part of the first floor. Since there is no parapet to the terrace, or other protection from the straight drop to the pedestrian area below, the access for taking a photograph was a little difficult. Nonetheless, thanks are due to the flat tenant for his co-operation.

There is a yet more disturbing theory about this statue: that it exists to curse everyone. A magazine article in 1988 developed this idea by citing the big increase in vandalism and litter at that time, and the general devastation before the building of the new Sovereign Centre. The question was posed: 'Has the Devil's curse at last laid its claws on this former spa and rival to Bournemouth?' The people were exhorted to fight the Devil's curse and make Boscombe as important and prosperous as it was in the past.

Laurel and Hardy had planned to come to the UK for a vacation but, when director Hal Roach saw the adoring crowds, he persuaded them to do a tour. The Boscombe performance took place in the week commencing 11 August 1947, and was reported in the *Bournemouth Daily Echo* the next day, under the heading 'Hippodrome Audience Set Rocking':

> Those two first-class slapstick comedians, Stan Laurel and Oliver Hardy, last evening had the large audience at the Boscombe Hippodrome rocking with laughter from the time they made their appearance until their exit.
>
> For the majority of people, it was the first time they had seen these popular screen comedians in person and the event was regarded with some importance by both young and old.
>
> For nearly half-an-hour Stan and Oliver delighted the audience with their simple but cleverly-timed actions, such as have amused millions of cinemagoers, Oliver acting as the man of some importance and Stan as the 'big cry baby'. They were assisted in their laughter-making by Harry Moreny.
>
> There is a first-class supporting bill, which includes dancers, a comic pianist, spring bed, acrobats and a flying trapeze act.

Although it is not the same in cold print, part of the performance is worth describing in the hope that imagination can do the rest. Originally written by Stan Laurel for a Red Cross benefit in 1940, the Driver's Licence Sketch was expanded for the 1947 British tour. In the sketch, Ollie has inherited a driver's licence from his grandfather and now wants to renew it with a cop. The latter asks what the 'N' stands for in the name Oliver N. Hardy and is told that 'N' is for 'Enry' and you spell 'Holiver' with a 'Ho'! The cop insists that you don't write Henry with an 'N', to which Stan replies, 'Of course you don't. You write it with a pencil.' When asked why the address has changed, the answer is, 'Because the landlord wouldn't raise the rent,' only for Stan to add, 'Well we couldn't raise it could we Ollie.' It also comes to light that Ollie has a driving conviction for speeding – on the pavement.

The cop decides to test Oliver on his road sense, outlining at great length a hypothetical emergency in which a choice must be made to hit either an ambulance or a train. During the cop's speech, Stan and Ollie are helping themselves to his packed lunch. 'Now!' declares the cop as the startled pair spit crackers everywhere, 'Which one would you hit?' Stan reasonably chooses the train as they would need the ambulance for getting home. In true Fred Karno style, the cop refuses the licence, picks up a shotgun to chase them off and trips over Ollie's cane, sending buckshot into the air. 'Why don't you watch where you're shooting?' shouts Ollie.

Some visual gags were included, such as Stan's hand, adorned with a finger splint, jerking into the policeman's face and dislodging his hat – naturally, the hat was replaced by Ollie the wrong way round. Ulverston Laurel & Hardy Museum say that the sketch took on a new life in performance, as evidenced by the volume of the laughs audible in a rare sound recording.

Since the Hippodrome was then in the same ownership as the imposing Chine Hotel nearby, the performing actors naturally tended to stay there, Laurel and Hardy being no exception. The illustration shows them with the proprietor, Fred Butterworth, (father of present owner John) in the hotel kitchen, in a typical pose with a dumb Laurel and a soon-to-be if not already exasperated Hardy. Judging by the laughter on the face of the kitchen staff, there must have been a gag just before the photograph was taken. It is just one of an amazing gallery of photographs on permanent display at the hotel – a veritable who's who of the theatre world.

Laurel and Hardy on a national tour in 1947
Laurel and Hardy stayed at the Chine Hotel and were photographed with the proprietor, Fred Butterworth. However, unlike for all the other nationally famous artistes in the hotel's gallery, their picture had to be a comic shot taken in the kitchen. (Courtesy of the Chine Hotel)

And finally, the ghosts. Reports include a clown seen floating across the ground floor, a lone member of staff hearing applause from the balcony before locking up, and a girl seen running along the length of the back bar before disappearing. A team of paranormal investigators who spent the night there in January 2006 reported temperatures dropping without cause, electromagnetic activity, small stones being thrown and a strange blurring red light showing fast movement. Some said the ghosts were stirred up by the building works.

Entertainment fashions have clearly been reflected in the varying uses of this playhouse since the end of the nineteenth century. Probably, a minority of these fashions would have been regarded by some of the Victorians as morally uplifting. We can only hope that there is no real curse on Boscombe …

FOUR

Oldest House Imponderable

*I*t is surprisingly difficult to answer the question: 'Which is the oldest house in Bournemouth?' For a town universally acknowledged to be extremely new, one might expect to avoid the hackneyed excuse of: 'Sadly, it is all lost in the mists of time.' Nonetheless, the discussion here may serve as a brief introduction and possibly prompt some more research.

There are some doubts about those early properties in the town centre. Tregonwell's new house, called the Mansion (Fig. 5), occupied in 1812, may have been built just after his butler's cottage. The Tapps Arms, in Old Christchurch Road, was 'established' in 1809 but it is unclear if and when Tregonwell rebuilt it later. In addition, little is known about some houses which he appears to have bought, together with the Tapps Arms, in 1812. These were seemingly purchased on the understanding that Tapps (the Lord of the Manor) would erect no building to 'annoy the view of the present houses'. These may be the houses shown on the 1845 engraving of the view from Prospect Mount, shown in Chapter Six. Cliff Cottage, where the Bournemouth International Centre now stands, could go back to any time from 1810 to 1815. There is also uncertainty over the use of Bourn House, which is shown on the 1759 map extract in Chapter 20 at the location of today's Debenhams. Of those mentioned so far, only part of the Mansion survives, within the Royal Exeter Hotel.

If we look outside the centre, other large houses do predate the Mansion – Littledown House (c. 1798, now part of J.P. Morgan), Stourfield House (1766, long since redeveloped), Iford House (1795) and Boscombe Cottage (c. 1801, although largely rebuilt after 1850 and now Shelley Park). Moreover, there were mulberry trees at the Boscombe site, which were considered in 1910 to date back to the Stuarts (1603-1714) and were thought to imply some form of residence at that time. Indeed, just behind the main building, there is still a tree which almost certainly was propagated from one of the 10,000 mulberry trees planted around the country by James I, when he was trying to use them to create a viable silk-worm business. Mulberries are usually propagated by 'planting' a branch of an existing specimen: roots develop, so creating a new tree.

In 1947, the *Echo* reported that the Ranger's Cottage (at the Old Barn near Hengistbury Head) may have been the oldest house, due to what looked like a date marked on a roof rafter (1537). However, such a mark is not definitive and that building is not likely to date from before the eighteenth century. Nonetheless, since it appears on maps of 1759, 1777 and 1785, we can say that it is the oldest building considered so far and still standing, except for one thing – it is not known when the residential part was converted out of the main barn. But should we be discussing this one at all, bearing in mind it was only brought into Bournemouth by the 1931 borough extension? By that time, the town had grown to about ten times its 1856 area. As the 1931 boundaries are now long-standing, the current town area has been used for the purpose of this chapter.

The plot thickens when we look at the ancient small villages that are close to the river Stour and which now fall within the Bournemouth boundary – Throop, Muscliff, Ensbury, Kinson, Holdenhurst, Iford, Tuckton and Wick. The Christchurch Inclosure Award of 1805 also predates the founder's Mansion and officially reveals eighty-six cottages; when were they built? It is probable that some remain to this day. Pelhams House (*c.* 1793), Ensbury Lodge and Primrose Cottages are all eighteenth century, and no doubt there are other examples. In 1780, the notorious smuggler, Isaac Gulliver, purchased the elegant Georgian house Howe Lodge in Kinson, but that was demolished in the 1950s. Wick House on Wick Lane is listed as dating to around 1800.

Faced with such a welter of evidence about the many houses predating those of the founder, how are we to decide on the oldest large house? There is one which stands out as a major contender due to its age: Ensbury Manor (*see* Chapter Twenty-seven). Part of it was built at least 750 years ago, making it the oldest in town – provided one is happy to consider a property demolished before the Second World War. If not, the longest surviving large house may be one not yet mentioned: Kinson Manor Farmhouse, as illustrated. Listed in 1952 as Kinson Farm, this two-storey house dates from around 1700. Apparently, it used to be a pair of cottages, and the front wall was

Kinson Manor Farmhouse, c. 1700
A contender for the present town's oldest house. (Author's collection)

'The Shack', Throop
Probably the oldest house yet found, 'The Shack' may well pre-date Shakespeare. (Author's collection)

rendered because the tile-hanging was at the end of its life. It was most unusual because those tiles were made to look like bricks.

There is yet another house to consider, the oldest of all. 'The Shack' is located towards the river end of Broadway Lane in Throop – as quaint a thatched cottage as any you will find. Its official Grade II listing refers to the sixteenth century, whilst one historian has dated the inglenook fireplace to the fifteenth century.

When the Tregonwells established their summer retreat at the Mansion they were not really the first residents, but, in the mores of the day, they were the first that 'counted'. One thing is clear: there were some large, and many small, houses on the site of present-day Bournemouth at the time of its foundation as a watering place in 1810.

FIVE

Labrador, Police and Pond

T he reader may agree that Labradors are a type of dog with a keen sense of humour, or perhaps one should say with a keen sense of fun, especially where water is concerned. In this instance, there was just such a dog, but with extra attributes – a knowledge of how to manipulate the fire brigade, the police and Bournemouth Borough Council.

It all began at the side of a pond on Turbary Common, when a black dog set up a tremendous howling from early in the morning of 16 April 1974. As can be seen from the photograph, this is a heathland of rough scrub, trees and grass ideal for dog owners. Being a Local Nature Reserve, Turbary Common has a management plan

Dead Dogs' Scrub, Turbary Common
A black Labrador caused the council to fill in a dangerous pond at this spot. (Author's collection)

whereby the council divide it up into compartments, which each have a programme for suitable maintenance and improvement as necessary. Having consulted with the council, the most likely pond where the howling occurred was in Compartment 6, known as 'Dead Dogs' Scrub'. The track in the picture runs north-east from Downey Close, whilst the pond was on its left before a change of direction. As can be seen, the former pond is an area now covered by trees and bushes. Gypsy John Doe is quoted as saying: 'They drowned so many dogs in there that they named it Dog Pond. If any dogs had to be destroyed they went in there.'

The first reported witness of the disturbance was a man from nearby Maclean Road. Police and firemen were called and naturally speculated about the possibility of a body under the water. No doubt the dog was inconsolable. Indeed, more than once the police had tried to lead it away from the pond, but it kept returning with renewed howls. If there had been foul play and a corpse was there, it was felt that it should be established without delay. The canine manipulation had begun …

The Labrador duly watched with interest whilst the pond was drained by the fire brigade – and then disappeared. Although plenty of dumped rubbish was found, there was no body. People looked around: 'Where's that dog?' But he had gone. The focus shifted to identifying the dog's owner but without success. His work was done and he had escaped.

Yet he was not purely a humorist. After all, this howling technique drew the council's attention to the unsafe nature of the pond; it was filled in and this source of danger to the local children was removed. Was this his real objective? Whilst one might say that he was wasting public resources by fruitless scaremongering, the better opinion might be that his heart was in the right place. Not only that, but is there not a lesson for us all here? That direct action has merit when trying to make an impact on the decision-making process of local government?

SIX

Tregonwell and his Great Accidental Invention

Whenever Bournemouth's foundation is considered, Lewis Tregonwell is invariably described as the 1810 founder, a status historically endorsed by the council with the huge centenary celebrations in 1910 and some bicentenary celebrations in 2010. He is painted as a rather dashing and aristocratic soldier, but is this exciting picture of the town's origin strictly correct? Although there is some justification, it is certainly not a simple matter of a determined pioneer establishing a colony in order to make a new town on previously unused land – rather, he began a new phase in the history of the area. The best assessment may be that referred to on his family vault in St Peter's churchyard, where it is stated: 'BOURNEMOUTH, which Mr Tregonwell was the first to bring into notice as a Watering place by erecting a Mansion for his own occupation …' The dictionary definition for the word foundation is the 'act of setting up, establishing etc.' – that would certainly relate well to the vault's inscription, provided that the words 'as a Watering place' are added when he is described as founder. However, these additional words are generally omitted in this book to avoid tiresome repetition.

What was this man like and how did he inadvertently start to create one of the fastest growing towns in the country? Particular thanks are due to two direct descendants of Lewis and his second wife Henrietta, six generations down the line: Sir Mervyn Medlycott, who has researched the family history in such detail, and Mrs Julia Smith, who kindly agreed for me to photograph his 1798 portrait by Thomas Beach (Fig.6). Incidentally, it seems that on one occasion there was a party from Bournemouth Borough inspecting the portrait at Edmondsham House. When Mrs Smith was asked by a member if the picture was a copy of the one held at the Town Hall, she had to reply that it was the other way around because she has the original and the council has the copy – that was given to the Commissioners in 1890 by the widow of Lewis's son, John Tregonwell (1811–1885).

Early Life of Lewis Dymoke Grosvenor Tregonwell (1758-1832)

The large, aristocratic and wealthy family can trace its history back to Milton Abbas at the start of the sixteenth century and indeed even earlier to Cornwall. Lewis was born in Anderson, Dorset, went to Oxford University, left without a degree (which was not unusual then) and proceeded to lead an active and rather wild life. Until his middle years, the tendency was to dissipate the family fortune and, when money ran short, to secure some more of it and carry on as before – he was either a winsome adventurer or a mixture of shrewd ambition and profligacy.

An early success was his appointment as High Sheriff of Dorset when he was just twenty-two years old. Another was his first marriage in 1781 to Katherine, the sole child of the wealthy Sydenhams – it followed his 'application' for her after she was advertised by her domineering mother for £100,000! Despite his property both on inheritance from his father (who died when he was just three years old) and from the marriage settlement, the couple kept overspending and then asking her father, St Barbe Sydenham, for more money. In the end, his mother-in-law became so exasperated, and relations were so bad, that he decided he 'needed space' and took his family to France in 1787. But it was only a temporary solution because the high life continued and he returned the next year to replenish funds. By some reports, his mother-in-law had prevailed upon her weak husband to give no more money to the young couple and, for good measure, to disinherit Katherine. Lewis determined to take direct action.

The chosen method was to go with his family to the home of his in-laws and invite St Barbe outside to see his daughter and grandchildren in the carriage. He was always keen to keep in with his father-in-law, who held the purse strings and after whom he named a son. Having then got his companions to forcibly bundle the old man into the carriage, Lewis locked up his mother-in-law and a footman, before stealing a horse and fleeing the scene. When the abduction came to court, St Barbe told the judge he would sooner live with his daughter's family; Tregonwell's victory was complete. Indeed, was it more of a rescue than an abduction all along? A modest settlement was made for the devastated Mrs Sydenham. Lewis bought Cranborne Lodge, the spendthrift life continued, and the main Sydenham fortune was reputedly run down even more. Although both Katherine and her brokenhearted mother died in 1794, St Barbe made over two manors to his son-in-law the following year and died in 1799. The next year Lewis married another heiress, Henrietta.

After the death of Katherine and before his marriage to Henrietta, Lewis joined Dorset Volunteer Rangers in 1797. As captain of the Cranborne Troop, he was charged with preventing smuggling and defending the section of coastline from Poole to Bourne Chine if Napoleon should attempt to invade. But was he involved in the smuggling trade himself? There is only circumstantial evidence. For example, when it was necessary to demolish his butler's house, Symes' Cottage (later known as Portman Lodge after Henrietta's family), there was an interesting discovery. A substantial cellar was found 3ft below ground level and had trap door access only – was it an ice house or was it for contraband? If it was the latter, that could have been the work of Symes alone. Again, the implications in the satire by Mrs Drax Grosvenor (see Chapter Nine) about tubs of liquor stored underwater could have been humour only. Moreover, the fact that most people from all levels of society seemed to have been involved in the Free Trade at that time does not prove that Tregonwell was amongst them.

As with Katherine, he was to have three children by Henrietta. John, born in 1811, became a most respected Bournemouth Commissioner under the Bournemouth

Portman Lodge, formerly Symes' Cottage, Exeter Road, 1856
Originally built for the butler Symes, this house (the most prominent building in the engraving) was later extended and occupied by the Tregonwells. (Courtesy of Bournemouth Libraries)

Improvement Act of 1856, and oversaw much of the town's runaway success. According to a plaque in the Cranborne Church of St Mary and St Bartholomew, on John's death in 1885, the family of Tregonwell became extinct in the male line. John had been born and died in Cranborne Lodge, the property bought by his father Lewis, using the Sydenham money. A window was dedicated to John by his widow and three daughters with the legend: 'Come unto me all ye that labour and are heavy laden and I will give you rest.' Although John inherited the estate, he died without male issue. The valuable town centre land was thus inherited by his nephew, Hector Munro, under the terms of Henrietta's will.

Prince Regent and Cherry Brandy

A great contemporary was the famously high-living Prince Regent, who became George IV in 1820. On one occasion, when Lewis Tregonwell had less than a day's warning of his visit to Cranborne, he was most anxious to have available a bottle of cherry brandy, which was known to be a great weakness of the Prince as an after-dinner drink. The shocked housekeeper managed to plan a good dinner at short notice whilst the master searched for some cherry brandy. Fortunately, a former Mistress of the Robes to the princesses happened to be living in Cranborne at that time and, being noted for her excellent cherry brandy, provided a bottle at once.

Following a perfectly acceptable meal, the time came for an after-dinner drink and Lewis personally poured his important guest a glass, yet the Prince Regent took one sip only and set it down without comment. On leaving the room, the host asked his butler to put the glass to one side. Afterwards, the question over the single sip was solved – the maker of cherry brandy was also proficient at making writing ink, which had been supplied by mistake and made a disgusting drink!

Pre-Tregonwell Bournemouth

Was there anything here, and did anything happen before his time? The answer is a definite yes! This limits Tregonwell's contribution to the founding of the watering place, which was initially called Bourne by local people (older people still called it that before 1900). Certainly, there is current recognition that he did not found it single-handedly, because the new plaques on the Pavilion include no less than seven other founders who are stated to have 'pioneered the founding of Bournemouth 1805–1860'. Slightly surprisingly, the smuggler Isaac Gulliver is amongst them. There were also some large houses in enormous sites no doubt bustling with the usual full complement of servants, e.g. Stourfield House, Kinson Farm, Pelhams House, Boscombe Cottage, Iford House, Littledown House and Ensbury Manor.

In considering the question of when Bournemouth began, it is probably a little extreme to go back to pre-history, but nonetheless, the site of the present town has provided substantial evidence of ancient human occupation. Flints, barrows, artefacts, etc. have been discovered, proving Stone Age (Old, Middle and New), Bronze Age and Iron Age camps and settlements, including one of the first true towns in the country at Hengistbury Head. Moving swiftly on to Tudor times, it is right to say that whilst Poole and Christchurch were established towns, the use of land in between was sparse. Indeed, current Bournemouth was once known as Stourfield Chase, and was administered on the orders of Henry VIII from Christchurch Castle.

The main track from Christchurch to Poole followed the line of the present Christchurch Road and Poole Road, crossing the Bourne Stream at the present Square. Other current main roads of the town follow the line of the old tracks used by a variety of people – travellers, smugglers, gypsies and sea-bathing parties. The undeveloped heath was sometimes crossed by fishermen, who would have lookouts on the cliff tops in order to direct the boats to mackerel shoals in the bay.

On the north side of the present town, the land was much more suited to agricultural use, being lower and more fertile along the river Stour; the villages of Iford and Holdenhurst date back hundreds of years. Not only was there normal arable and pasture, but also the farmers turned out their animals for summer grazing onto the common heathland to the south. Commons rights were most important, particularly for the unofficial occupiers. Small thatched huts were occupied by families, eking out a rather precarious existence on the common. Some were gypsies, known as 'diddycoys'. Rights of turbary allowed them to cut peat, heather and gorse for fuel; many kept beehives and they were able, in a limited way, to pasture animals for food. Rabbits and fish were an important part of their diet. These people were not really supposed to be there, having no formal arrangements with the Lord of the Manor. Accordingly, there was little official recognition of their existence in the Christchurch Inclosure Award of 1805.

However, the Award made considerable arrangements for what might be called the official occupiers. Although nearly 5,100 acres were enclosed, covering most of the present town, five large sites were set aside to be used by commoners. A well-trusted farmer, William West, lobbied successfully on their behalf for a reasonable amount of replacement land. As the town developed, the right to cut fuel was no longer needed and these areas were allocated instead for recreation. They are now known as Redhill Park, Meyrick Park, Seafield Gardens, King's Park and Queen's Park. By an Act of 1889, concerning Meyrick Park, compensation was due to the occupiers of fifty-eight cottages for loss of turbary rights, and agreed at a total of £500.

In summary, before the 'founding date' of 1810, the heathland, and some agricultural land of present-day Bournemouth, had been used for many years. Though sparse, the population included farmers, commoners in their cottages, and a few large houses. Land-dealing and pine-planting had been facilitated by the 1805 Award, meaning that conditions were right for a new health resort to spring up. Lewis Tregonwell showed the way by putting up some of the first buildings in what is now the town centre.

The Tragedy and the Visit to Bourne Chine

By the time he remarried in 1800, Lewis's wilder days were behind him. One can imagine this to be true from the 1798 portrait in Fig.6, or does he rather show an air of weary melancholy? He was now leading the life of a country gentleman in a state of domesticity rather than that of a young adventurer. Henrietta's first child, also named Henrietta, was born in 1802 and her second, named Grosvenor Portman, in 1807. Sadly, he was dead within weeks.

The circumstances of the death were truly awful. In the middle of a family party, the guests were distracted by what has been described as a frightful bellowing coming from the baby's cradle. Henrietta tried to settle him with a soothing ointment, unaware that the nurse had already used this remedy without effect. The second dose was thought to be the cause of death. The mother's distress at being the instrument of her son's death can hardly be conceived.

By now, the invasion fear had been mainly removed by Nelson's defeat of the French at Trafalgar in 1805 and Lewis was no longer in the Dorset Volunteer Rangers. By all accounts, he was anxious to lift his wife out of her depression. When they were staying at Mudeford in July 1810, he decided to show her Bourne Chine, already familiar to him from his time patrolling the coast. On riding out there, she was totally captivated by it as a place for a summer residence. That year, he bought some 8.5 acres from the Lord of the Manor, Sir George Ivison Tapps, at about £20 per acre and built the Mansion. Although the identification is not free from doubt, Fig.7 is believed to depict Tapps – the portrait certainly shows a man of shrewd appearance. The sea air, beautiful surroundings and tranquillity did indeed bring back Henrietta's contentment. More land purchases, new cottages, tree planting and visits by the Tregonwell circle followed.

Creation of Bourne Tregonwell

Lewis and Henrietta made a success of their new summer retreat, which initially included just the Mansion and a cottage for their butler, Symes. Although it is not the generally accepted opinion, there is some evidence that Symes' Cottage was actually built first. After many alterations and changes of occupation, the greatly enlarged

Mansion has become the Royal Exeter Hotel. The first change was the letting to the Marchioness of Exeter in 1820 – hence the name of both house and road. Fig. 5 is a side view of the hotel now, with an inset of the original Mansion. Symes' Cottage, later called Portman Lodge, was on land later used for the Hants & Dorset Bus Station, which burnt down in 1974 and is now a car park by the Square.

Terrace Cottage was erected opposite for the gardener, who looked after an orchard behind what is now Primark. Altogether, about 36 acres were bought from Sir George Ivison Tapps to the west of the Bourne Stream, and a few detached holiday homes were built. The Tapps Arms on a site of nearly 4 acres was acquired in 1812 and became the Tregonwell Arms at what is now Post Office Road. The site, which included more than one house when bought, was sold by Henrietta to the licensee after Lewis died in 1832. Yet for about twenty-three years after Lewis and Henrietta first occupied the Mansion in 1812, there was virtually no competing development from outside the tiny village informally named Bourne Tregonwell. The 1835 map extract (*see* Chapter Eighteen) shows how little had been done by then. It became the playground of the Tregonwells, their friends, relations, and those taking holiday lets. Moreover, early Bourne apparently wanted to keep everything very select, and opposed commercial premises in principle – after all, goods and services could always be provided by Poole and Christchurch tradesmen.

Having seen the potential of the founder's village, Tapps-Gervis (Tapps' son) pressed ahead with his own plans in 1836. After Lewis had shown the way on a small scale, he was determined to use his better land on the east side of the Bourne Stream for a much bigger development scheme, including sixteen villas in Westover Road and the Bath Hotel. The Prospect Mount engraving gives a view from widow Henrietta's

View from Prospect Mount on West Cliff in 1845
St Peter's Church, Westover Road villas, Bath Hotel, Belle Vue Hotel, Tregonwell Arms and nearby cottages can all be seen; otherwise it is trees and heath. (Courtesy of Bournemouth Libraries)

high land on the West Cliff in 1845. Most of the buildings shown were on Tapps–Gervis' land and had only been erected since 1835. Once John Tregonwell inherited in 1846, the west side was more seriously promoted. From that time forward, the development of the town was assured, because the centre had two main owners who were keen to see growth.

Exhumed and Reburied

When he died in 1832, Lewis was buried at Anderson, his ancestral home. After years of living quietly with Henrietta in Cranborne and Portman Lodge, his wild early days must have been a distant memory. She had a monument erected to him in the form of an urn on top of a massive pedestal in Cranborne Gardens, which became the Winter Gardens site. An 1859 map still shows the raised mound. However, as time went on, she became unhappy about his place of rest. His re-interment in a family vault at St Peter's Church in central Bournemouth took place just a few weeks before she died in 1846, no doubt relieved that it had been possible to make the arrangements in time. She did not forget her infant son Grosvenor, who was re-interred on the same day as his father. It must have been an emotional occasion.

The watering place known as Bournemouth was thus accidentally invented in 1810 as a result of the heartbreaking death of a baby in 1807. It was not the foundation of a town so much as an attempt to aid a wife's recovery from severe depression. It seems very fitting that mother, father and son are all now laid to rest in a family vault close to the centre of the embryo town, known in 1835 as Bourne Tregonwell.

SEVEN

Bard of Bournemouth

Cumberland Clark was a man of many parts. According to his autobiography, he suffered smallpox at the age of six, cruelty and starvation at his boys' school and the general condemnation of his teachers. Having been close to death three times before the age of twelve, Clark's various jobs and travels were astonishing – pioneer missionary taking open-air services in an Australian gold field; backing himself to win as a racing jockey; being at different times a sheep drover and hunter with dingoes; and owning and running an 800-acre wheat farm in Canada. Despite being an adventurer and fighting the Aborigines in Australia, he still had a great respect for their traditions. His experiences and anecdotes of life were legion. However, he is mainly known in Bournemouth for raising the art of doggerel to a new level, one which is a joy to read. There follow a number of verse extracts from the *Bournemouth Song Book* – extracts which need 'reading out loud in a jaunty manner'. Without more ado, an example about air:

> *The Bournemouth Air*
> There's something about the Bournemouth air.
> That acts on the scalp and forces the hair,
> That reddens the cheeks and makes them tingle,
> Marries off people who are single.
> Why do the flappers wear short frocks and make the fellow stare?
> There's not a doubt about it – it's the Bournemouth air.

In order perhaps to establish his affection for the town, the next extract makes clear that there is nothing it cannot do on the medical front.

> *Bournemouth – The Cure-All*
> It is a magnificent cure-all,
> For illnesses single or plural,
> Every want you'll find it supplying –
> A fact that but very few folks are denying.
> So roll down to Bournemouth as fast as you please;

Shed all your trouble, and live at your ease.
Of all the good things it possesses the most;
No other place like it is found on the coast.

But Clark did not confine himself to Bournemouth alone – like Shakespeare (more of which later), he considered matters beyond these shores, as now shown.

Bournemouth and Napoleon
Now Captain Lewis Tregonwell, a Briton bold was he,
Who in the famous Dorset Rangers held a Captaincy.
To him the duty was assigned the British Coast to watch,
From Purbeck to the Bourne Chine, and old Bony's plans to scotch.
He did the job in first-class style, I'm led to understand,
And didn't give the enemy an earthly chance to land.
I hope it isn't too late as I the story tell,
To give three hearty cheers for Captain Lewis Tregonwell.

Although he is relentlessly cheerful and positive when dealing with pine trees, some philistines have coined the expression 'magnificently bad' to describe his works and could therefore have decided that the pines were not health-giving after all – a sad loss of image for the town.

The Pines
So inhale the Pine scent; for I'm sure if you care to,
You'll find it'll cure all the ills flesh is heir to,
Erase the grog blossoms that bloom on the nose,
Faulty complexions, or bunions on toes.
Here's my advice – take a walk on the Cliff:
To cure all your troubles, just stand there – and SNIFF!

This might be a good stage at which to take a step back and wonder if he really was a truly bad poet. This man came through the days of music hall and variety, when popular entertainment was a straightforward affair of catchy tunes, simple stories and sentimentality. It has been suggested to me that the explanation for the 'bad verse' is twofold. Firstly, it was never intended to be taken seriously and secondly, Clark wrote the poems to music in his head – hence their description as songs, not poems. The next example takes us to Canada, where he really was writing the lyrics for music.

He provided some verses for a merry song about the feared monster of Lake Okanagan, in British Columbia. According to Indian legend, the water demon, N'ha-a-itk, required a live sacrifice to provide safe passage; his island shore was believed by many to be littered with the gory remains of those not meeting his requirement. Cumberland Clark rose to the challenge by writing the lyrics for what became a music hall hit in 1924: 'The Ogo-Pogo: The Funny Fox-Trot.' It not only succeeded in changing the name of the monster to Ogo-Pogo, but also removed the fear element. Reports of monster attacks fell off dramatically and instead, local people looked in a more curious and kindly way on the creature. These are some of his words which did the trick:

> I'm looking for the Ogo-Pogo
> That funny little Ogo-Pogo.
> His mother was an earwig, his father was a whale,
> And I want to put a little salt on his tail.
> I want to find the Ogo-Pogo while he's playing on his old banjo.
> For the Lord Mayor of London, the Lord Mayor of London, wants to put him in the Lord
> Mayor's show.

For anyone interested in hearing it, there is a rendition of the song with the Paul Whiteman orchestra, albeit with minor changes to the lyrics (the website address is: www.youtube.com/watch?v=uQE8T6Ip6Ic). By such means, the Bournemouth Bard seems to have laughed out of existence a mythical monster of the deep.

The next instance may best be thought of as mind over matter, or maybe 'you only have TB – snap out of it!' When promoting itself as a 'select health resort', the embryo town named a path through the pine trees by Westover Road as the Invalids' Walk. However, did Clark simply have no time for what he might consider the raving hypochondriac?

> *The Invalids' Walk*
> But please do not think in the Invalids' Walk,
> You only meet 'Crocks' – that's ridiculous talk.
> To be strictly impartial and honest and just,
> I *must* say frequenters look very robust.
> You see no collapses or faints; they seem to possess no complaints.
> The average face by enjoyment is lit,
> And everyone looks to be perfectly fit.

The final verse extract clinches Cumberland Clark's credentials as a ladies' man.

> *Bournemouth Girls*
> As stated, they win many hearts, as Beatrice captured Dante.
> (The clothing worn by Beatrice though, perhaps, was not so scanty.)
> But really they're so nice,
> You can't help looking twice.
> Such visions, too, of limb –
> Your eyesight's much too dim!
> I don't seek contradictions, as a rule, but still I'll risk it,
> And say right here, for lovely girls old Bournemouth takes the biscuit.

These extracts are but a tiny proportion of Cumberland Clark's publications, yet the *Song Book* was enough to earn him that title of great prestige – the Bard of Bournemouth.

Cumberland Clark (1862–1941), Bard of Bournemouth
Although his poetry has understandably been criticised, Clark was a scholar, writer and man of many achievements.

The reason could be that he has managed to brighten the day of many a reader, at the same time as being accused of 'gouging a rhyme out of any crevice'. The chances are that he was both aware of and amused by his local reputation, whilst all along knowing he was not being fairly assessed.

So what of his achievements beyond poetry? He found time to write seventy-two books, with particular emphasis on the British Empire, Shakespeare and Dickens. They covered such diverse subjects as coins, national flags, the curse of Communism, the British Empire at war, New Zealand, Australia, India and Canada. In a three-day sale in January 1914, Sotheby's auctioned off his collection of mainly Greek coins, amounting to 392 lots. In recognition of his work on Shakespeare (including some 2,000 slides to accompany lectures), he served as president of both the Shakespeare Society London and the Bournemouth Shakespeare Society. In addition, he belonged to the Zoological Society, the Royal Geographical Society and the Royal Astronomical Society.

Cumberland Clark was an intellectual, a practical man of great energy, and a humorist. In his time, he was attacked with spears, nearly starved in New Zealand, and made the mistake of buying a fake gold mine. This last loss-making venture involved a vendor who simply put some gold into the earth sides of the mine,

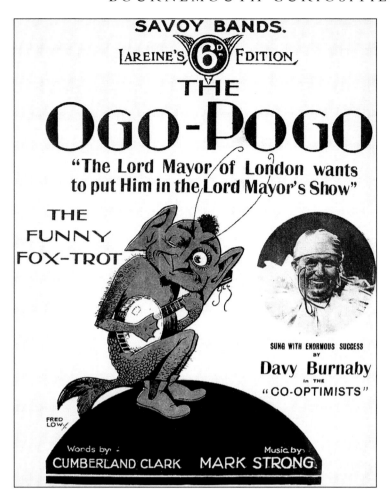

The Ogo-Pogo:
The Funny Fox-Trot
Cumberland Clark
wrote the words to
this enormous music
hall success of 1924.

thereby falsely inflating its value. After the death of his wife in 1933, when he was seventy-one years old, he moved from London to Bournemouth. His first premises had a study with an outstanding view high above the Palace Court Hotel – perhaps it is understandable that he felt it was an 'earthly paradise'.

I have had the good fortune to speak with a gentleman, Michael Doland, who was a boy of just six years old when he knew Cumberland Clark. He came to the town with his mother in 1935 and recalls their friendship the following year. In particular, Clark impressed his mother as a distinguished mature gentleman and was always kind to the young lad. Smiling one day in 1936 as he walked towards their beach hut from Bournemouth Pier, he was clad in a dark blue overcoat with a curly black fur collar and wearing a bowler hat. The overall impact was enhanced by the walrus moustache, silk scarf, ebony stick, be-spatted feet and yellow gloves. While Michael's mother made the writer and poet comfortable in a folding chair, with the aid of a plaid car rug, the boy was asked how he was that day and patted on the head. The eminence (as Michael now refers to him) had no difficulty in charming, against the odds, another habitually frosty member of the family who happened to be present at this unexpected meeting. In brief, this eyewitness account is all about kindness and mannered gentility.

Michael's opinions on Clark's poetry may perhaps be influenced by his gratitude to a thoughtful gentleman who helped out his family at a very difficult time. Nonetheless, he considers the writing should certainly not be scorned due to its sometimes tortured verse, bearing in mind it contains much well-observed social comment – it could thus be described as 'sub-Betjemanesque'.

Unhappily, towards the natural end of an incredibly full and charmed life, Clark's luck finally ran out. He was living at a block of flats (which is still there) known as Fern Bank, St Stephen's Road, when killed by a direct hit on the night of 10 April 1941. It was just three minutes to midnight and the stick of bombs in the vicinity of the Square damaged 112 properties, leaving eight dead altogether: seven women and Cumberland Clark. A three-man rescue team dug a tunnel through debris at Fern Bank for nearly six hours to rescue a trapped woman – they were later highly commended for this dangerous work. Clark had already written his own epitaph: 'The longer I live the more do I turn to Christianity as the one hope for salvation, the one faith for the soul of man, the one comfort in distress, and the one consolation in death.'

Cumberland Clark deserves to be remembered for a lot more than some humorous poetry that does not scan too well.

EIGHT

Pine Trees –
The Great Enablers

The resort has been famous for pine trees from the earliest stages of its development. They were publicised in two phases: firstly, to stress their health-giving properties in the earlier days of the visitor seeking convalescence, and, secondly, to stress their beauty in the later days of the ordinary seaside visitor. As the town changed from helping the 'recuperation of the well-off' to the great 'holiday by the sea', so the pines were re-marketed. There was even a train titled the Pines Express, which ran from Manchester to Bournemouth from 1927 to 1967. Were the enormous plantations started with a view to enabling expansion as a health resort, or was that a welcome and unexpected by-product of cash-cropping the timber? Probably the latter, but, however that may be, without these trees Bournemouth would not have grown as successfully as it did. Thus the crest of English roses above the shield on the borough's coat of arms, granted in 1891, is surmounted by a pine tree.

Early Days

The pines were triggered to a large degree by the Christchurch Inclosure Award of 1805, which provided landowners with sufficient legal interests to plant the trees on the former commons. Naturally, the planting programme varied over time in terms of locations and speed. However, one might say that it was fast and furious during the nineteenth century and the sheer attraction of the trees helped the huge resort-based development over that period. But how did all this come about? And is it not ironic that the Great Enablers were greatly cut down to allow the resort to be built? It has been estimated that some three million were planted by the time borough status was achieved in 1890, but now, due mainly to urbanisation, there are less than 100,000 left.

The natural state of the country, in the absence of man's intervention, is dictated by soil, climate and local sources of seed. If humans were to disappear, many open areas of arable and pasture land would be colonised by the trees. However, the presence of mankind changes everything. For instance, when Bronze Age farmers cleared the trees from light soiled areas, heathlands developed, leading to an expansion of heather and associated species. Extensive sheep grazing can also restrict new woods

Bournemouth coat of arms at BIC
The pine tree's importance to the town is recognised by placing it at the top of the arms. (Author's collection)

developing. Historically, farmers have removed trees to realise the value of timber and to create rough pasture. Hence, the 'high land' of the town (around 100ft above sea level) shown on the old maps as Bourne Heath or Pool Heath, was actually converted from forest to heath by the actions of mankind over the centuries. Since it was common land subject to some grazing before the Award, and with few trees to provide seed, its return to woodland before the 'arrival' of Bournemouth was only slowly and sporadically progressing.

Thus by 1805, historic tree felling had left most of present-day Bournemouth as a rather desolate heath, with a few areas of woodland and some scattered trees. Five years later, the founder's wife, Henrietta, was hugely attracted to the wooded Bourne Chine as an idyllic location to spend the summers. The evidence suggests that, consistent with this, they planted trees in those early years for amenity reasons. By the time of his death in 1832, Lewis Tregonwell had acquired some land west of the Bourne Stream and developed it to an area of extremely low-density housing for use as holiday homes. There were open areas, an orchard, the viewing point Prospect Mount and a very large clear area south-east of the Mansion (Fig. 5) allowing an open outlook to the sea. Cranborne Gardens were laid out and an area set aside for archery. There is nothing to indicate that he wanted to have his own pine plantation for a distant future cash crop.

Meanwhile, Sir George Ivison Tapps, the Lord of the Manor of Christchurch, had been planting enormous numbers of pines over his estate, one which had become, in effect, 1,149 acres larger, thanks both to the 1805 Award and his low-cost purchases under it. This was a remarkably favourable measure both to him and, even more so, to his successors in title. It is probable that having secured a freehold interest with vacant possession in the land, he simply wanted timber as a cash crop, knowing that it was too poor for arable or adequate grazing. Moreover, he seemed to resist development of his own land. But it remains possible that he was speculating for development value in the long term, on the principle that, if he was wrong, at least there would be a commercial timber crop to be had. An argument against the speculation theory is that he would have used an amenity tree-planting scheme had that been the real objective. One simply does not create a dense pine wood in order to have amenity trees for property development in the future. Yet even that claim could be rebutted – after all, it worked very well in practice.

Land was offered for sale in 1803 and 1804 in a way which indicated both potential tree schemes and land speculation. Some 300 acres of 'heath ground' by the current Holdenhurst Road (and allocated to Lord Malmesbury) was offered for sale or to let in 1803 as suitable for both turnips and tree planting. It is likely that the claim for it being turnip land was optimistic, suggesting, as it does, deeper soil. Less than a month later, in 1804, a somewhat larger area at the same location appeared for sale in lots, one of which (44 acres) referred to more arable crops such as corn and carrots being possible. There were fine views of the Needles and beautiful country, and this time building potential was hinted at by the expression 'well worth the attention of gentlemen to build upon'. Sir George Tapps had planted trees on his land in the closing years of the eighteenth century. By 1788 Edmund Bott had provided pines at Stourfield House, which was advertised for sale in 1789 as including flourishing plantations. As the house was bought by Tapps, he would have managed those plantations first hand. Suffice it to say that in 1805, the obvious crop was a pine plantation but there were slight stirrings about the possibility of valuable building development.

By the time of his death in 1835, Tapps had built just one property – the Tapps Arms in 1809. However, the potential of the area must have become clearer, because by 1836 his son was planning the building of the sixteen villas in Westover Road and the Bath Hotel. Before coming into his inheritance as Lord of the Manor, he must have been impressed by the success of Bourne Tregonwell. From then on, the scent and general appeal of the pine trees became a top marketing feature for the town. What might in today's jargon be the 'unique selling point' took many forms: the strong endorsement by the watering place expert, Dr Granville; the constant use of the expression 'health-giving properties'; the claimed beneficial effects of the pines on the micro-climate, causing warm winter temperatures in the chines, and so on.

It is likely that the present town's pine planting was carried out in four broad phases. Firstly, we have the existing trees before the 1805 Award, comprising partly experimental, limited planting and partly self-seeded. The landscape would have been mainly heath with sporadic trees and some woods. Secondly, at an increasing rate after the Award, Tapps and other owners started their own tree schemes as commercial plantations. Thirdly, from 1810, the founder began with amenity planting (excluding any building site and its curtilage) on his newly acquired land in order to provide an attractive tree-lined environment for his future village. Finally, mass planting was carried out on Award lands.

It is worth taking a moment to see the big picture. The strange thing is that whilst the town might have been created anyway, it was mainly chance which enabled it at the time. The Award of 1805 had given a solid foundation for the future Bournemouth. Although enclosures to aid agriculture had been taking place for a long time, it was by a dubious method of local agreement that Parliament disliked. The threat from Napoleon gave a fresh impetus, because action was needed to have more and better farming for the survival of the country. Parliament duly recognised this situation by passing a general enabling Act in 1801 to simplify the whole complicated process. No doubt that encouraged Tapps and his fellow petitioners to push for the 1802 Act that led to the 1805 Award. However, since the heath was generally too poor for arable or pasture, tree plantations were the only real agricultural improvement option under the Act. (For completeness, it should be mentioned that difficult though it was to work the land, some arable farms existed on the high part of the town at West Cliff, Boscombe, Winton and Moordown.) As the pines became so popular, it is not too far-fetched to say that the war effort against Napoleon was partly responsible for creating the premier seaside resort of Bournemouth.

The start of the town, as a watering place, followed from the famous 1810 visit of Lewis and Henrietta to the wooded and undeveloped Bourne Chine. Having built houses for himself and his butler, Lewis probably planted trees to provide a pleasant environment for his visiting friends, family and holiday tenants, and it was only Tapps' son who had the real vision. His vigorous building work from 1836 to his death in 1842 promoted the health benefit of the pines in what was called the Marine Village of Bourne. As the resort took off in the second half of the century, the pines played a big part in its success, despite many being felled to allow new buildings.

Remarkable Pine Trees

Fig.8 is an example of a pine wood under management by Bournemouth Council. Pugs Hole Local Nature Reserve at Glenferness Avenue has fairly mature trees which show how the vast tracts of land would have appeared to a walker going from Boscombe to the East Cliff in the middle of the nineteenth century. In low-density residential areas such as Talbot Woods (Fig.9), the wide roads, with generous pavements and shrubberies, allow the retention of tree strips with all their high amenity value.

Bare land can be planted with pine saplings at 2,500 per hectare, implying that 1,200 hectares would be used to tally with the 1890 report of three million trees in the town. Since the 1805 Inclosure Award dealt with over 5,000 acres (about

2,000 hectares), that amount of planting is perfectly feasible. However, the need for selective thinning over time means that after several such harvests, the final trees standing would be spaced at perhaps 100 to 200 per hectare, just 4 to 8 per cent of the original number. This provides each of them with 50 to 100 square metres of space. Since few pines live for more than 100 years (when they would typically be 1m diameter), any plantation is a constantly changing picture of tree numbers and volume of commercial timber per hectare. After a slow start, timber growth speeds up and then declines towards maturity. A good level of production for pines would average about 7.5 cubic metres of new timber per hectare per annum. No doubt these are the sort of calculations carried out by the estate manager for Sir George Ivison Tapps and other beneficiaries of the Award in 1805.

A typical rotation length would be about seventy years for a plantation. This could explain the common myth in some quarters that Bournemouth pine planting did not begin in any numbers until about 1870. It has to be a myth because there are numerous historical text references to plantations being created on a large scale after the 1805 Award. Maps and photographs exist in support of such references. Hence, there could have been many old trees removed for development and even more harvested by 1870, and the new ones would only date back to that time. To be clear, the rotation length of seventy years is not an invariable rule because it tends to apply to commercial forestry owing to competition, disease and harvesting. Indeed, digressing to a very rare case, there is a bristlecone pine in America that is over 4,750 years old – it has been named Methuselah. At the start of the twentieth century, around 10,000 trees a year were reportedly being planted in Bournemouth, perhaps in replacement for, or adding to, those along the big roads. Today, the council's planting figure is much less than 100 standard pines (1.5 to 2m high) a year on a mainly replacement basis, only in the town centre, along the roads and in the formal gardens.

The Bournemouth soil conditions on the high land are suitable to these trees, being acid and sandy with some clay. The four most common tree types are maritime (or Bournemouth) pine, Scots pine, Monterey pine and varieties of black pine (Corsican, Austrian and Crimean). The fast-growing Monterey is a Californian import, which can add up to 6cm to its girth every year while it is still young. Strangely, the Bournemouth pine is now the least common, though many could have been lost due to the work of the pine shoot moth, which burrows into new shoots and either kills the leading shoot or undermines the shoot. It then collapses and, as it re-grows, introduces a kink into the stem shape. The Monterey and maritime pines have the great disadvantage (to us) of having large heavy cones that have been known to dent cars. The black pines often line the avenues of the town and are quite common in the remains of the woodlands, e.g. Pugs Hole, Redhill, Queen's Park and Meyrick Park.

As a generality, the south of the town has been found more suitable for pines and the north for deciduous trees. Moreover, the Scots pine has been found less resilient to drought ground conditions than the maritime pine – this is not surprising considering that the first hails from Scotland and the second from the Mediterranean. However, the 'Scotties', as they are known in the business, can usually still manage here, albeit often slow-growing – they can take sixty years to reach a diameter of 25cm, yet sometimes become enormous. A topical management issue for local authorities is to decide how many new trees are needed, bearing in mind the growth of the existing stock, which of itself adds timber every year. Although the aforementioned seventy years applies to commercial plantations, individual trees can live for much longer. For example, after one blew down in the 2009/2010 winter on the roadside quite near to Wick Ferry, an old photograph was found showing it as a mature tree in 1913 – the stump and remains look like it could date back around 200 years. The relic is so unusual and important that a plaque may be placed there by the council.

Pine can be used as general-purpose softwood for carpentry, telegraph poles, pit props, railway sleepers, etc. Turpentine, made from pine trees, is an important substance that has many applications, including uses for cosmetics, solvents and pharmacy. But are there real health benefits for the convalescent, as boldly stated by the developers and doctors of the growing town? Since these trees do take some pollutants and carbon dioxide out of the air and give back oxygen, that exchange must be an advantage, as perhaps is the slightly heady aroma of pine resin. Who is to say that any sense of well-being, perhaps arising from the pine scent, is really a placebo effect? To keep some balance here, we should not overlook the point that pines do emit volatile organic compounds (VOCs), which may be harmful to humans either on their own or in combination with man-made pollutants.

A good example of 'pines adoration' is provided by Sir James Clark, Queen Victoria's physician and Bournemouth resident. He praised the influence of the pine woods, saying they should be preserved and that a certain number of trees kept whenever land was taken for building; he considered that they were 'among Bournemouth's best doctors'. Many felt likewise. One critic, however, was Farmer Dale of Tuckton, who, reminiscing in 1871, greatly mourned the loss of the heath, the bees and the sea breezes blowing over the cliff and plateau. He said that the new woodland was much less healthy due to rotting wood and fungus, and that local inhabitants were dying younger as a result. However, this example is scarcely evidence-based and is enormously swamped by the number of those saying the opposite at that time.

The pines are no longer a strong selling point for the town – they have mainly gone due to the very success of the town's building programme, which required large-scale felling. Now that the resin scent has all but disappeared, we are left with a unique treescape that includes residual pine trees along main roads instead of something more usual, such as lime trees. Nevertheless, a feeling for old Bournemouth can still be experienced by walking along a chine or roads such as Manor Road, East Cliff (Fig. 14). But people can no longer be delighted with the turpentine scent of pine trees when walking on the main pier because there are so few left. Does it matter that they have mainly disappeared? Perhaps with a streak of ruthlessness, the great and the good of the town would reply, 'No.' They realise that it is no longer necessary to attract the rich wanting a health cure – all credit to the Great Enablers for helping the growth of Bournemouth, but they always were dispensable.

Yet there remains a postscript to the story: it could be that the virtues of the pines will be increasingly recognised again, but for different reasons. Both urban change and warmer, stormier weather will alter the living and working conditions of the town.

Pine Walk by Bourne Stream in the Lower Gardens
Formerly called 'Invalids' Walk', this was an important part of Bournemouth's appeal to the convalescent.
(Author's collection)

Trees like the pine provide a natural method of modifying such conditions for everyone's benefit. Urban temperatures are modified by reducing the 'heat island effect'. Trees do this by shading surfaces, sheltering areas and releasing moisture into the air. They moderate flood levels by soaking up water, filter out pollutants and are a source of daytime oxygen. Other advantages to the urban scene include stress reduction, providing a link with nature, marking the seasons and creating wildlife habitats. Hence, Bournemouth still needs its trees and should have a clear plan to sustain them forever.

NINE

Bourne Takes a Joke in 1816

One of the earliest houses to be built at Bourne was Cliff Cottage, occupied by the aristocratic Drax Grosvenors of Charborough Park. It is believed that this thatched cottage was erected between 1810 and 1815. Around the same time, the Mansion was built by Lewis Tregonwell and then occupied by his family in 1812. The families were friends and neighbours in their large Dorset houses, and must have sociably agreed to have nearby summer residences at Bourne Chine. Certainly, according to an 1801 document, both Tregonwell and Grosvenor were captains in the Dorset Volunteer Rangers, with commands of forty and seventy-five troops respectively.

Mrs Sarah Frances Erle Drax Grosvenor wrote a short play in 1816, entitled *A Peep into Futurity*. If that is any guide, she must have been a cheerful, witty and possibly even mischievous personality. Although it claims to be looking at how Bourne will be in 1876 (hence the title), it is nonetheless an extremely rare glimpse into the very early days when it was written. It is a quirky, disjointed document, with a lack of dramatic continuity but with the benefit of some explanatory sketches. Almost certainly, the supposedly 1876 characters shown in the illustrations relate closely to the 1816 ones, and are, almost without exception, outlandish or ridiculous and sometimes both. We shall never know if they all took the satire in good part at the time or whether some of them were smiling through gritted teeth, so to speak.

Eternal themes are explored, such as the giddy nature of young men set on wooing, and the different viewpoints of fathers and would-be fashionable daughters. Other things are less definite, such as the introduction, which refers to something perching on Sarah's chimney top that was nearly blown away in the recent whirlwind and was a 'sort of mitre at top to prevent smoak'. This sounds like an early type of chimney cowl which looked like a bishop's headdress. She writes to the 'Most Excellent Governor' as 'Old Gypsey of Meg's Hill' and 'thy occult adviser in times of sickness' – it is all very whimsical.

The social whirl of the well-off should be kept in mind. For example, an August 1813 press report described the tremendous Monday night entertainment provided before the start of the Blandford Races on Tuesday. Mr and Mrs Drax Grosvenor and family attended the very spirited balls. At 2 a.m. on the Tuesday, the company moved on to the Crown Inn for the steward's supper and excellent wines. Songs, duets, glee, good humour and dancing continued to between 5 a.m. and 6 a.m. – competition indeed for the entertainment potential of tiny Bourne.

An alternative title for the play was given as 'Small talk at Bourne some sixty years hence, between the Dandies and Elegantes of the day'. It was 'humbly dedicated' to 'His Excellency the Governor', which can only mean Lewis Tregonwell, who was about fifty-eight years old in 1816 and possibly, in her eyes, overly magisterial in bearing. Whether the play was acted or read, one can visualise this happening either at Lewis's Mansion or Grosvenor's Cliff Cottage. It is simpler to understand the play itself if we first become familiar with the illustrations.

Sketches to Accompany the Play

The first picture depicts the townscape now (1816) and in the future (1876). At the earlier time, there are just two buildings – one on the East Cliff and one on the West Cliff. There is also a rickety footbridge over the Bourne Stream. At the later time, a quite prophetic vision is given: hotels, marketplace, castle, assembly rooms, bazaar, coffee house, tea gardens, theatre, church, gaol, boarding school for young ladies and 'new bridge over the river Bourne by the voluntary subscriptions of the fashionable residents of this distinguished and frequented bathing place'.

Our first 'people sketch' has Lady Delia Desperate attended by Frank Flourish and Jack Splatterdash 'a la King's Cushion' (Fig. 10). In the play, she is criticised by Miss Penelope Parasite for setting a new fashion of being carried up and down the sandy cliffs near to the Royal Tea Gardens by her humble admirers. Whilst Delia in transit is smiling happily, the Elegantes were angry, presumably because they had been upstaged. A 'King's Cushion' is a temporary seat formed by two persons crossing their hands, with the person being carried placing their arms around the necks of the carriers.

Lady Delia has two gawky daughters, the elder being Miss Julia Desperate. Sir Sampson Puff, a rich City Knight, has come to Bourne to seek a smart wife from

Penelope and Lady Georgina 'Degage'
Two Bourne belles are extremely relaxed on a summer morning. (Courtesy of Mrs Julia Smith)

amongst the Bourne belles, and one or more of the Desperate women had managed to throw a pannier over his back so that Julia could sit on him (Fig. 10). The drawing has him on all fours whilst she is side-saddle on the pannier, with a fan directed at and cooling his head. Penelope says he is dying for that 'hoyden' (meaning a wild, boisterous girl). Another sketch has the two gossipers, Penelope and Lady Georgina Gossamer, lounging at ease on a summer morning and 'degage' (meaning uninvolved, free and relaxed in manner). Such was the anticipated small talk of 1876. The play does not contain a plot as such but rather a description of activities, conversations and the culture of the day.

Our next illustration has the elderly John Tregonwell of 1876 (Lewis's son) sitting on a bench in front of Russell's Circulating Library on the Esplanade Paradise Row, talking with his daughter Miss Harriet (Fig. 11). The picture goes with Scene Three. He wants her to see a bit of the *beau-monde* (fashionable society) and enjoy the breezes of the cool evening. In a boat nearby, the dinner guests of the hotel behind the bench are being entertained by Venetian boating songs. John explains where 'the old gypsey lived on yonder cliff', i.e. the present West Cliff, and how his parents (Lewis and Henrietta) would often consult her by moonlight. Elsewhere, we learn that her name is Meg Merrilees. But the old man is failing to communicate his reminiscences about the Bourne of sixty years ago to his daughter, who says she 'cares not a pin for these horrid stories of witches and owls and midnight vigils at the gypsey's lovely cliff sixty years ago'. She then makes her demand to go to a grand ball at Evans House, but he insists upon her wearing a 'good old fashioned petticoat not cut shorter than mid-leg'. He was not able to approve of the new fashions: 'Why child! 'Tis downright indecent.' Miss Harriet exclaims, 'Oh the cross old square toes!' and exits crying.

The last two illustrations have been left to the end of this section because they do not relate to the play itself; it could be that some of the play has now disappeared, or that it was never fully written. At least that would explain the absence of plot. The start of the manuscript does advise that it is 'meant as a frontispiece to a new work now in hand …'. Suffice it to say that these two sketches deal with smuggling, whilst the play (or play extract) does not.

The first one shows the seaward end of Bourne Chine and the excitement associated with three kegs: two of them at the feet of the Governor and his wife, and one still offshore in a rowing boat. Next to the two kegs is written the Bournists' motto: 'Spirits from the Deep Arise! Oh! Arise!' These words surely refer to the raising of tubs of brandy etc. from the underwater hiding places used by smugglers. Meanwhile, the Governor sings: 'Blow high blow low; Let tempests tear; The main mast from the hold.' Not content with bringing ashore the hidden tubs, the Governor (of Cornish ancestry we must remember) may be hankering for a spot of wrecking. Both he and his wife are dressed for a south-west gale and are taking a drink. A young Bournist holding her hand is 'in his cups'. The largest character is rushing down the West Cliff, knife in hand, with the legend: 'The wild Cottager flying to catch a breaker well armed in case of a Bandit.' It is significant that 'breaker' has two meanings – a wave and a keg, the latter being an evolution of the contemporary Spanish word *bareca*. At the top of the cliff is a driver with donkey and cart, ready to go over the edge, noted as 'The Bourne charioteer urging her steed to flight'.

Cliff Cottage, West Cliff, on the site now occupied by the BIC
The Drax Grosvenors' quaint cottage. Unlike the inland site of Tregonwell's Mansion, the site of Cliff Cottage had a long cliff frontage. (Courtesy of Bournemouth Libraries)

The final picture (Fig. 12) is a little difficult to read and interpret but the general idea is clear. After a storm, there is a rush by all and sundry to carry away contraband. Tregonwell's wife is trying to hold him back from the race to the shore: 'Oh: stop Governor you are too Eager.' Was she reminding him of an old-established pact to turn a blind eye and leave the risk-taking to the smugglers' landing party? His reply implies that the wild cottager is ahead of them, as he urges his wife to 'run my dear and never mind your nose'. There are several references to 'sea weed', which could mean smuggled tobacco. The natives are stated to be 'engaged in civil war in collecting the treasures from the deep'. As a cottage has tumbled down in the storm and it is 'more work for me', that could refer to Cliff Cottage, where the Drax Grosvenors lived.

The Governor's heavy horse has a loaded cart and 'is taking it coolly'. Time is clearly of the essence because one note says: 'Cottagers racers at a Long gallop for Seaweeds' and a cottager is shouting, 'Now for New Market gallop my boys.' An exhortation is given: 'Make haste man and get another load', bringing the protest: 'I am running with all speed we shall get all the sea has thrown up.' Although a comic creation, it is easy to see *A Peep into Futurity* as yet more circumstantial evidence of the town's founder being involved in the Free Trade.

Play of Three Scenes

The first scene has two dandies struggling with matters of love. Frank bemoans being 'done over completely' due to his confounded waltzing with the fat Dowager Heavy Sides till six this morning. Yet he still manages to hope a particular lively lady will 'sport her neat little ankle tonight'. Jack cares not, concerned as he is about having to 'raffle by proxy' for three duchesses and a 'little heiress', who even then approaches at full gallop, a cue for Frank to go to play tennis by the New Bridge.

In Scene Two, Elegantes Georgina and Penelope talk at much greater length than did the Dandies. They discuss fashions, ladies' wear and millinery, matters medical and other people. A major concern is whether to 'drop' the fashionable 'passe-partout' (a muslin petticoat) which 'incommodes' Georgina on the hot sands. Penelope is in favour of starting a new Bourne fashion, in this way reminding her companion of Delia's new fashion last year, which 'made us all die of anger', being the King's Cushion. The pannier and Sir Sampson Puff are described, as is the cackling voice of a singer of Italian songs.

It is also suggested that, in former times, the old gypsy Meg would lay snares and pitfalls on her cliffs to catch any Poole belles straying there on a Sunday with short petticoats. Georgina becomes fatigued and wants Dr Grosvenor, Meg's grandson, to be called to feel her pulse, yet changes her mind as he deals too much in 'simples' (ignorant or common persons) and 'evacuates too much for me'. Tellingly, when referring to the founder's Mansion in former times, Georgina remarks that it was then considered a 'lonely and rather desolate spot, the only neighbours were a gang of gypseys and smugglers'. The much-mentioned gypsy Meg Merrilees is clearly taken from Sir Walter Scott's *Guy Mannering*, and perhaps the poem by John Keats. It may even be that the character was chosen by the authoress because the poem gives such a good portrayal of the bleak Bourne of 1816.

Scene Three relates closely to the father/daughter sketch. It was that common human situation, a dialogue of the deaf. The old man, John Tregonwell, was interested in tradition and nostalgia, whilst his sprightly daughter was living more in the present. He was seeing again in his mind's eye how 'wild and romantic' the cliff (West Cliff) once looked, whilst now (1876) it was noisy and dirty. In contrast, she thought only about the ball being held that night in honour of Princess Leopoldina.

Although the play's characters are established, we have no clear plot and there are no lines to explain the smuggling sketches. This has been mentioned to two descendants of Lewis Tregonwell (one of whom has the original manuscript), but neither can throw any further light on the matter. It could be that some pages are missing, or that the satirical whimsy was taken to the point of leaving it incomplete on purpose. However, there is a sad postscript.

In 1822, some six years after writing this work, 53-year-old Sarah Grosvenor (now a widow of three years) was riding in her carriage through Hammersmith when her groom and coachman were grossly assaulted by a fellow who attempted to get up behind the carriage. After a desperate resistance, he was secured. When the matter came to court, he made a most affecting plea to her for mercy on the grounds of humanity to his wife and children. The report states that it was indeed so affecting that she fell into the arms of a servant in a fit and soon became convulsed. By the time that medical aid could be obtained, she was a corpse owing to an 'ossification of the heart'. The medical view at the time was that her heart had turned to bone.

TEN

Shopwalkers, Package Transport and Father Christmas

eales, the town-centre department store, has been one of the town's many success stories and a well-documented one at that. This chapter looks at just three unexpected aspects of the firm's 'culture in practice', which perhaps go some way towards explaining that success.

Shopwalkers were a Victorian phenomenon designed by the retailers of the day to ensure maximum business. The idea was almost to intimidate the customer into making a purchase! It may have suited the very well-off, who appreciated the personal touch and recognition of status. But it must have been a little unpleasant for the impecunious casual shopper – today it seems bizarre. The famous retail magnate from Chicago, Gordon Selfridge (who, in passing, planned a castle on Hengistbury Head), understood this very well. But his reforms, to make the shopping experience fun for all, were ground-breaking in this country. As the following extract from a booklet (*see* Bibliography) about the Beale family's expansion demonstrates, it was not just Selfridge who was ahead of his time:

> Usually dressed in a tail-coat jacket and striped trousers, at least until the First World War, the shopwalker, whilst he had certain supervisory and managerial duties, was also a rather glorified usher. It was his task to welcome customers, recognising the well-known ones, and to conduct them from their carriages to the appropriate counter. John Beale remembers that nearly all the departments had 'bays' of counters arranged to form a hollow square, with stock fixtures in the middle. Each counter had a least one chair on the outside, to which the customer was conducted by the shopwalker who would then call an assistant forward to serve. If a sale was not made it was usual for the shopwalker to enquire why this had not occurred and it was normal in most shops to regard the failure to 'make a sale' as a matter for reproach. John Beale, however, also remembers that his grandfather was very advanced for his day for his comment in such circumstances was always 'Never mind if you didn't make a sale – the important question is, did you make a friend?' This question throws a great deal of light on the methods and beliefs of J.E. Beale.

It is common knowledge that retailing has always been hard work and unforgiving on the feet of the shop assistants. Since pay levels have hardly been exceptional rewards for the tiring days, it counts for a lot if members of staff at least feel that they are part of one big happy family. Beales seems to have fostered this sense of contentment more than most. There is a saying that 'leadership is one part telling, one part showing and one part doing'. In other words, if the staff can see that those in charge are taking part in the more arduous or unpopular tasks, morale will be boosted. Package transport is a good example.

As the firm expanded and sales increased, there was a need to hold more stock. The extensions of 1906 enabled upper floors to be used for this purpose. Large deliveries arrived on a regular basis in the days before goods lifts. They could easily have been viewed as a dreaded chore but it was a case of 'all hands to the pump', including management. After the cases were unpacked, members of staff were arranged as a human chain up the stairs in the form of a relay. All the able-bodied males and the younger girls passed each box from hand to hand. Mr Bennett Beale usually got a tall pair of steps and stood on the top, passing parcels over the banisters. It is a little difficult to work out exactly how this 'shortened the angle of the stairs' as reported, but one gets the general idea. Including rest breaks, one or two tons could be stored in about an hour. How much better than designating a few unlucky people to climb the stairs for ages!

Beales always had a Father Christmas for the children, but the store took the facility to new heights in 1912, by commissioning one of the new aeroplanes. It was just two years since the 1910 Bournemouth Aviation Meeting and the sadly fatal crash of Charles Stewart Rolls, co-founder of Rolls-Royce. Moreover, that week had seen other crashes and serious injuries of aviators. Realising, therefore, that putting Father Christmas into an aeroplane in winter was a dangerous idea, Cyril Beale decided to do it personally. It happened that the *Daily Mail* was organising a Tour of Britain by air,

Beales' Father Christmas was flown over the town in 1912
A great stir was caused by Cyril Beale personally waving to the crowds from the aircraft and later arriving at the store in a coach and four. (Courtesy of the Beales Archive)

and the newspaper was persuaded to have the Beales Father Christmas as one leg of it. In the absence of operational local aerodromes at the time, a search was made for the largest and most level field that could be used. In the end, take-off took place at Four Elms Farm, Iford, which was at the bottom of Pokesdown Hill.

At first, the famous pilot Henri Salmet took the plane and his eminent passenger low over the promenade between Boscombe and Bournemouth. A little later, they were cheered from the rooftops over the town. Father Christmas's robe, beard and locks were streaming in the wind. As the pilot flew low over the store, he waved from the cockpit at the crowds below. Since this is not a conventional outfit to exclude the extreme cold of open-air flying in mid-winter, it is not surprising that his cheeks were blue and his nose was red on landing in Meyrick Park. There, a small boy accepted a teddy bear, thanked the pilot for bringing Father Christmas safely to Bournemouth, and added that he too wished to fly but that would have to wait until after Christmas. Cyril was soon ensconced on the top of a coach drawn by four horses and attended by a brass band. People cheered the coach on its way into town and the Beales store – what an experience!

Nigel Beale has given me an extra insight into the picture. Does it seem a little odd that Father Christmas has no hat? Yes. Is that perhaps due to it being a windy flight? No. The truth is that it was a well-established Beales tradition for him to have no hat, a tradition that lasted from the very start of the business to the time when Beales discontinued having a Father Christmas. When the firm's founder was planning to move from his job in Weymouth to start up in Gervis Place, Bournemouth, his employer delayed matters by reminding him of the need to give six months' notice. Thus Nigel's great-grandmother opened up the store, rather than his great-grandfather, and Christmas intervened before he could join her. However, when creating the outfit, she could not, for the life of her, 'get the hat right' – so the very first Beales Father Christmas had to perform without one and so it continued ever after!

Just seven years later, at Christmas 1919, many members of staff returning from the horrors of the First World War were welcomed by a copperplate-style letter written by four members of the Beale family. To give an extract:

> It has been a great pleasure to watch the return during the last twelve months of those members of the Staff who have been absent on Active Service. Once more we are like the re-united family, full of reminiscence and anecdote and the spirit of comradeship. And so forgetting the trying times behind us all let us look to the dawn; the day breaks and all the future is ours.
>
> It is the sincere wish of the Directors that this Christmastime may have nothing but happiness in store for you and that the New Year may bring to you and yours a heart's content and each day its token of joys that will enable you to 'travel hopefully' throughout the year.

A different era indeed.

ELEVEN

Of Lightning and Ashes

Howe's Chronicles for 1613 tell the sad story of the death of a carpenter after a lightning strike on Holdenhurst:

Fire from Heaven burning the body of one J. Hitchell of Holnehurst.

Hitchell, a carpenter had been at work at the house of John Dean, of Parley Court, and returning home on Saturday eve, went to bed with his wife and young child. At midnight there happened a great and sodaine lightning. Hitchell's wife was upon a sodaine very grievously burned all the one side of her, and her husband and child lay dead close by her, but perceiving that her husband still burned inwardly, she drew him out of bed, and brought him into the open street, where through the vehenency of the fire she was constrained to forsake him, and he lay burning on the earth for the space of ye three days. There was no outward appearance of fire, but only a kind of smoke and glowing heat ascending from his body untill it was quite consumed to ashes, except only some small pieces of his bones which some of the sad beholders cast into a pit made neere the place.

A separate report was made in 1613 in a pamphlet by John Hilliard, entitled 'Fire from Heaven burning the body of one J. Hitchell of Holnehurst, in the Parish of Christchurch, in the County of Southampton, on 26th June 1613'. Extra information was included: he had truly and painfully laboured at his trade that day; his mother-in-law Agnes Russell had been awoken by a terrible blow on her cheek and had cried out to her daughter and son-in-law for help; as there was no reply, she had gone to them and roused her daughter from sleep; as John Hitchell lay burning on the ground for the three days, there was no outward appearance of the fire that was consuming him, but only 'a kind of smoke ascending upwards from his carcase'. In 1609, 'Jo Hitchel' is mentioned in the Churchwardens' Accounts for his work on the Old Church, including expenses for 'Tymber, Boordes and Nayles'. It is likely that he was the carpenter who died strangely just four years later.

It seems from the report that Mrs Hitchell was lucky to survive the lightning strike with burns but that the enormous electric shock killed her child outright, as is common with lightning; there is no mention of continuing inward burning

Spontaneous human combustion in Bleak House
Charles Dickens believed in the phenomenon and made sure that the circumstances of Krook's death tallied with SHC reports. (Illustration by Phiz)

for the child, only the husband. Consistent with this, there is also no reference to the child's body being taken outside to lay on the ground. Although it seems there was only a kind of smoke and glowing heat arising from the body, Mrs Hitchell was wise to leave her husband outdoors if they lived, as was likely, in a small thatched cottage prone to fire risk at the best of times. The glowing heat resulted in the body turning to ashes over three days – an account which is typical for the reported and controversial cases of spontaneous human combustion (SHC).

One way in which this case differs from the typical SHC report is that, in Hitchell's case, the possible source of combustion (lightning) was both external and dramatic. Normally this does not apply with SHC. Yet due to certain differences between this and other cases of fire or lightning damage, his death was indeed more akin to SHC. For example, a normal fire (such as a building in flames) will blacken the skin and damage the body beneath it by working inwards, from the outside. The temperature of a lightning bolt can reach 30,000°C, but a strike occurs so swiftly that about two thirds of victims survive. SHC differs because the burning is internal by nature and there are often no flames to be seen. Thus, whilst lightning or normal fires can indeed cause severe internal damage, they do not slowly turn the victim's torso to ashes afterwards. A doctor has confirmed to me that lightning could cause death after a few days but not turn the body to cinders.

So far, we have seen that Hitchell's death was not like one caused by lightning but was similar to deaths commonly attributed to the bizarre observable fact of SHC. Intriguingly, Charles Dickens researched some thirty such cases and believed in the phenomenon. Thus he 'killed' Krook, one of his alcoholic characters in *Bleak House*, by this method. Unfortunately, the theories dreamt up to explain SHC are rather slim, e.g. poltergeist activity, static electricity, obesity, UFOs and divine intervention. Another idea, since discredited, was that an alcoholic person simply brushing past a flame would set light to flammable alcohol that had seeped into the skin. At the time, one writer bracketed Hitchell with two other cases, where one was an alcoholic and another dosed on camphor; it was not known whether the carpenter Hitchell was partial to strong drink. As they had all been struck by lightning, that was deemed to be the cause – the fact that the type of burning in Hitchell's case was unlike that caused by lightning was just brushed aside.

In particular, the argument was that the lightning had 'kindled the body's phosphoreal fire', an effect greatly enhanced by alcohol.

However, the favourite current explanation for SHC is the 'wick effect', whereby a person's clothing is said to operate like a candle wick into the fat of the body. Even if that did happen to Hitchell, it is still not a proper scientific explanation of how SHC works or why the temperature can get to be so high that human ashes are formed. Many will conclude that SHC is pure hokum anyway. On the other hand, since it is not known how lightning could cause the 'Hitchell effects', we must wait for a scientific breakthrough to provide the reason for the 1613 tragedy.

Unsatisfying though it may be, the only real conclusion about the curious death of Hitchell is that we simply do not know why his body slowly burned to ashes.

TWELVE

The Queen's Ancestor and Stourfield House

Edmund Bott built the large and impressive Stourfield House, Southbourne, in 1766 – many years before Lewis Tregonwell appeared on the scene to 'found' Bournemouth. He was a cheerful barrister and an intellectual, who sadly died in 1788 at only forty-eight years of age, with the mansion and large grounds then passing to three cousins. The house was erected on a mainly uninhabited heath, with views to the north and the Stour valley. The name is self-explanatory because there were fields all the way down the hill to more level land by the river Stour. Part of the story is about how the enormous house and land adapted over the years to increasing urbanisation – today there is but a tiny remnant left. The other part concerns the help it gave to Mary Eleanor Bowes, a direct ancestor of the Queen, at a time when she was suffering huge distress.

When new, the property had its own carriageway access from the main Christchurch to Poole road through open countryside. We must visualise riding a horse (or being in a horse-drawn vehicle) along tracks through open fields and heathland dominated by heather and gorse. If arriving from the Christchurch direction, we cross the river Stour at the old and narrow Iford Bridge by the tiny village of Iford, and climb Pokesdown Hill to the heath. An occasional cottage might be seen. A smaller track is taken on the left in the region of what is now Southbourne Road, until the mansion set in parkland comes into view. To its north, St Catherine's Hill and the Priory Church of Christchurch can be seen in the distance. To the south and east, we find open land to the cliffs and Hengistbury Head.

When Stourfield House was advertised for sale on behalf of the first owner's beneficiaries in 1789, it was described as having 450 acres, of which half was let out (with leases nearly expired) and half in hand. There were several farms, whilst the mansion's appurtenances included stables, kennels, a walled garden, fruit trees, flourishing plantations and a pleasure ground. The entirety was felt to be 'suitable for the immediate reception of a genteel family'. Being around two thirds of a square mile of mainly open land extending to the present Cranleigh Road, the site's appearance in 1789 could not be more different from today's residential area. Sir George Ivison Tapps bought it and let it out to a succession of tenants. An early tenant in 1795 was the famous Countess of Strathmore, who was seeking a place for peace and recuperation, and a home for her many pets.

The family tree of the monarchy shows that the Queen is a direct descendant of the well-educated and intellectual Mary Eleanor Bowes, the Countess of Strathmore and Kinghorne. When she married the 9th Earl of Strathmore and Kinghorne in 1767, it was just two days after her eighteenth birthday, and she was one of the richest heiresses in the country; some say the richest. Her father was a powerful northern coal magnate, whose lands were exploited for the coal boom and yielded tremendous profits. It is claimed that her ghost still haunts the great oaks at Gibside Hall near Gateshead, an estate which she loved in her younger days. By the time of the Earl's death of tuberculosis at sea nine years after the wedding, they had had five children, including Thomas, whose

Countess of Strathmore (1749-1800). Engraving of 1786
Known as the Unhappy Countess, the heiress Mary Eleanor Bowes spent her last days in Stourfield House.
(© Dean and Chapter of Westminster)

son, Thomas George, was the great-grandfather of Queen Elizabeth the Queen Mother.

As an extremely rich and attractive widow of just twenty-seven years old, Mary appeared to be an excellent proposition for an adventurer, and so it proved. The first marriage had been less than perfect, with the Countess realising she had nothing in common with her fiancé, but going ahead with the match anyway. Certainly, a life of domesticity on the Scottish estates did not suit such an educated person who spoke several languages. Even when he was close to death, the Earl tried to discourage her passionate interest in botany. She relieved her boredom in 1769 by writing a poetical high drama, the *Siege of Jerusalem*, a story of unrequited love.

Perhaps encouraged by the success of this publication, the Countess did not stay true to her husband, indulging in a libertine lifestyle. She had an affair with George Gray, arranged two abortions, and was pregnant by him a third time when the Earl died. Later, they became engaged. Then a certain Andrew Robinson Stoney (1747-1810), of Anglo-Irish extraction, wooed her away from Gray and won her hand by outright fraud. The rest of her days were so blighted by Stoney's ill-treatment that she became known as the Unhappy Countess; one might say she was too educated and rich for her own good. Although his name became Stoney Bowes, he is referred to as just Stoney in the following text.

Starting as he meant to go on, Stoney tricked Mary into her second marriage by organising a duel under false pretences. He first arranged for the publication of scandalous stories (which he is believed to have written himself) in the fashionable society paper the *Morning Post*. Unknown to her, Stoney was in cahoots with the editor.

Stourfield (later Douglas) House, Southbourne
Built by barrister Edmund Bott in 1766, the enormous mansion had many occupations, one of which is
indicated on this postcard from 1906.

Ostensibly to protect her good name he challenged the editor to a duel, at which Stoney appeared to be mortally wounded. As a 'dying wish', he asked for her hand and, swayed by the animal blood deceptively daubed on his person, she assented.

Stoney was a highly skilled manipulator who was magnetically attractive to women. The Countess believed the duped doctors when they told her he was about to die, and thought she would soon be free to remarry – wrong on both counts. Some reports say that he was carried into church for the 1777 wedding service on a stretcher. He then performed a 'miraculous' and fast recovery, closely followed by all kinds of ill-treatment of his new wife. She was locked in a closet and suffered regular rape, as did the maids – even prostitutes were invited into the home. It was a miserable existence, with all correspondence censured, food restricted and physical beatings. The gossips of Georgian England were well served by the trials and tribulations of the Unhappy Countess for many years. Her previous 'free and easy' lifestyle did not help her public image, nor did the law readily provide justice.

Blue plaque, Stourfield House, Southbourne
Official recognition is displayed of the occupation by the
Queen's ancestor. (Author's collection)

Stourfield House remnant, Southbourne
The porches, railings and steps are all that remain of the original mansion and its grounds of 450 acres.
(Author's collection)

The Countess's vast wealth was partly kept intact through family trusts, but was otherwise squandered on an epic scale. In 1785, when she sued for divorce, citing a horrifying list of misdemeanours, Stoney abducted her on horseback during an abnormally cold spell and kept her compliant with death threats. Being the captive of a fugitive travelling the country must have been a terrifying experience; rumour had it that he had killed his first wife. Although she had been her despicable husband's prisoner for eight years, he had become (for some of that time) both MP and High Sheriff of Durham. After a successful rescue from her husband and abductor, his actions again came to court.

Eventually, the law (albeit then based on a husband having excessive rights over a wife by current standards) came down on her side and she regained her freedom in 1789. It is said that the expression Stoney-Broke derives from this man, who eventually died at a debtors' prison. Having won the court case, Mary lived from 1792 at Purbrook Park, Hampshire, moving as a tenant to Stourfield House in 1795 until her death five years later. It seems that local people found the Countess to be very odd but readily accepted this curiosity on learning of her life. Her three sons visited only occasionally, but her two daughters (one from each marriage) lived with her in the grand house. There were servants, a companion and many pets, including dogs that each had a hot dinner every day. Her daughter by Stoney was greatly admired when she stayed on her horse as he attempted to roll in the Stour at Iford. Mary kindly sent out hot meals and beer to the men in the fields, and her final will made many presents to appreciative local people. Stoney's only son with her died while serving in the Royal Navy in 1807.

Mary came to Southbourne as a retreat from a tough life, one which included regular beatings from her second husband. It is said that she favoured Stourfield because she 'could live feeling she was out of the world'.

What became of the mansion and grounds after her death there in 1800? Following several more lettings, Stourfield House was sold in 1844 to William Popham. He demolished part, replaced a pitched roof with a flat one, and had the red brickwork rendered. The Popham family put the estate up for sale in the 1890s in various lots, with a view to realising development value. One of them was the fifteen acres known as New Park, being an area in front of the main house which had been mainly enclosed from the common by Edmund Bott and planted with trees. It is now the crescent-shaped New Park Road, lying between Southbourne Road and Southbourne Grove. Virtually the whole of the original estate has been a residential area for many years.

The main house was bought in 1894 to be converted into a grammar school, and was then resold in 1896 to be turned into the Wellington Hotel. In the event, it never actually opened as a hotel but was used as a sanatorium until 1923. When it changed hands at that time, the same use was continued by the Royal British Legion as Douglas House, until it was taken over as a hospital by the NHS in 1948. That use ceased in 1989 and it was finally demolished the following year. The upper portico, lower porch, stone stairs and railings were preserved, however, and can still be seen today; they are used as one access to a new, smaller building. The latest Douglas House is an NHS fifteen-bedroomed residential block nearby, which, at the time of writing, is up for sale or to let.

Apart from showing the link to the Queen's family tree, this tale provides an unexpected comparison between Stoney and Lewis Tregonwell, recognised founder of Bournemouth. Both of them were twice-married to heiresses, both carried out abductions for financial reasons and both had to answer for it in court. But the similarities end there because Stoney was imprisoned after his brutalities and Lewis won the day. Despite the abduction (or was it a rescue?), Tregonwell's rich father-in-law, Sydenham, told the judge that he wanted to leave his wife and live with his daughter's family. Indeed, Lewis's legacy was one of kindly remembrance unlike Stoney's legacy of horror.

Stourfield House was a prestigious but isolated property of special interest to the Countess of Strathmore when she desperately needed to continue her recovery from Stoney's brutality. It would be pleasant to think that her last five years were spent in reasonably happy retirement in an area later to be developed as Southbourne-on-Sea.

THIRTEEN

Satire on the Sands

efore the building of the Undercliff Drive, there was controversy about the use of the sands for entertainment. There could be photographers, refreshments, fruit sellers, vocalists, toy sellers, ice creams, Punch and Judy, and marionettes. For example, on Whit Monday in 1889, there were masses of people on both sides of the pier 'in all ages and apparently of all conditions of life'. A day trip to the seaside by train was extremely popular; the pier might take tolls from over 33,000 visitors on a single day. Although there had been a big increase in beach trading by 1889, it was always frowned upon by many who considered that the 'wrong sort' were being allowed to the fore. After all, they reasoned, the town was supposed to be select. 'A Visitor', who probably just wanted some beach facilities, wrote to the press in May 1875:

Crowded beach near to the pier, 1890
Before the promenade was built here in 1907, the sands and facilities by the pier were very popular with day trippers and others, especially on bank holidays. (Courtesy of Bournemouth Libraries)

I notice that my old acquaintance Down, the tobacconist at Wootton Place, Lansdowne Road, has once more pitched his tent on the sands, and seeks a licence at the hands of the Improvement Commissioners for the sale of light refreshments thereon. Outside the tent, which was erected on Monday night, the following notice was posted: 'This marquee has been established on the foreshore of this beach for four years for the sale of refreshments; and as soon as the Improvement Commissioners grant a licence for the sale of milk, ginger-beer, lemonade, soda-water, bath and other buns, &c., it will be opened with everything first rate at the lowest prices. – N.B. The marquee may be used for shelter in case of storms by the visitors in the beach.' It seems to me that if the Commissioners would sanction the ginger-beer effervescence of the marquee on the sands, they might have a little less gas to blow off at their periodical meetings.

Beach entertainment today
In little over a hundred years, we have progressed from daytrips by train to visit a beach fair on the sands to the huge Bournemouth Air Festival, featuring the magnificent Red Arrows. (Author's collection)

FOURTEEN

A Ukrainian and Two Kings on the Beach

krainian, John Suchomlin, was an extraordinary artist able to create the most remarkable sculptures in sand. Although he claimed that his materials were limited to sand, water and colour, the displays were both very lifelike and faithful to either the original people or the accepted opinion of how they must have looked. The latter comment refers to the uncanny similarity between classical religious paintings and his work in sand, much of which included biblical scenes. The durability of the models is explained by the use of a type of calcium-based wash known as kalsomine, which provided some hardness and a smooth finish. Some details of his remarkable life are given here as a context to the way in which he touched 1930s Bournemouth.

According to Australian local history reports, his biography has the romance and adventure of a bygone age when many people travelled enormously, simply in order to make a life. He certainly seems to have been his own man. Having left school at thirteen, he took jobs on a farm, in a botanical garden and then a hospital. After a 500km hike, he became a seaman on the Black Sea. Then another hike over the Caucasus Mountains took him to a job on a three-master in the Caspian Sea. Later, he fled the instability of Russia for Germany, visited Africa and Argentina as a seaman, worked at a leather factory in Germany whilst studying art, and then spent two years on a Russian warship. Having arrived back in Germany as a stowaway, he eventually obtained papers in his real name and worked his passage to Australia in 1911. Along the way, a British captain took pity on Suchomlin when he stowed away on a ship to Rotterdam. There was also identity confusion with a Russian revolutionary, requiring a further escape, this time to Norway. What a richness of experience by the age of just twenty-four – or was it more a case of hard work and survival?

After becoming an Australian citizen in 1913 and opening an art studio, he married a mayor's daughter, Elsie Mattingly, in a suburb of Adelaide. For the next thirteen years there must have been a spell of relative peace when he and Elsie had two sons and he painted three portraits of mayors for hanging in the council chambers. In 1926 he moved to Manly, Sydney, and began sand modelling in the footsteps of a previous sand modeller, William Page, who was retiring. Suchomlin continued to work there sporadically until 1941. Over time, it was found that a

John Suchomlin (1887-1974)
(Courtesy of Manly Library Local Studies)

Figure 1: Tregonwell and Creeke sculpture
An amusing depiction of two people greatly involved in the town's development. The founder seems smug at the Town Hall and Creeke seems thoughtful on the WC. (Author's collection)

Below Left: **Figure 2: Christopher Creeke, 1820-1886**
(Author's collection)

Below Right: **Figure 3: Lewis Tregonwell, 1758-1832**
(Author's collection)

Figure 4: Old and new at Grand Theatre and Pavilion, Boscombe
Even today, this magnificent Victorian playhouse retains some
original features, such as the restored ornamental balconies.
(Courtesy of O2 Academy)

Figure 5: Royal Exeter Hotel today, incorporating Tregonwell's Mansion of 1812
The founder's Mansion can still be identified as that part below the tower and a gabled
section on each side. It originally had three gables. (Courtesy of Bournemouth Libraries)

Figure 6: Lewis Tregonwell in 1798
Part of the portrait by Thomas Beach, painted when the founder was forty years old and a captain in the Dorset Rangers. (Courtesy of Mrs Julia Smith)

Figure 7: Sir George Ivison Tapps, 1753-1835
Part of a portrait believed to be the Lord of the Manor, who secured most of the present East Cliff under the 1805 Inclosure Award. (Courtesy of Sir George Meyrick)

Figure 8: Pugs Hole Local Nature Reserve
It was once possible to walk in Bournemouth for miles through this sort of scented idyllic woodland. (Author's collection)

Figure 9:
Street scene of pines in Talbot Woods
Wide roads permit the retention of these most attractive trees. (Author's collection)

Figure 10: King's Cushion and pannier
Two Bourne belles are indulging their amorous fancies: one to be carried up and down the sandy cliffs; the other to ride on the back of a City Knight. (Courtesy of Mrs Julia Smith)

Figure 11: Founder's son John Tregonwell (1811-1885) and John's daughter failing to agree
He rejects the latest fashion for a ball, whilst Italians are singing from a boat. (Courtesy of Mrs Julia Smith)

Figure 12: Contraband at Bourne Chine – A Peep into Futurity 1816 or 1876?
The inhabitants are rushing to get spirits and tobacco ashore and safely away. (Courtesy of Mrs Julia Smith)

Figure 13: Albany, East Cliff
The town's most prominent block of flats continues to attract both praise and criticism. (Author's collection)

Figure 14: View from roof of Albany to the east
Manor Road can be seen as a belt of trees running to Christchurch Road. (Author's collection)

Figure 15: Original fireman's pole within a students' bar at the Old Fire Station
At about 47ft, this is believed to be the country's longest fireman's pole. (Courtesy of Bournemouth University)

Figure 16: Town centre, 2007
A view from the Bournemouth Eye. (Author's collection)

Figure 17: Sewage pumping hall hidden below the Pier Approach
These are the pumps which send the town centre sewage uphill to Boscombe so that it may proceed by gravity to the works at Holdenhurst. (Courtesy of Wessex Water)

Figure 18: Hidden clock at St Peter's Church
Extensions to the church obscured the stunning 1848 timepiece and caused its relocation to this bell-ringers' chamber. (Author's collection)

Figure 19: Water tower in Upper Pleasure Gardens
Decimus Burton (1800-1881) built the tower to enable a fountain and irrigate flowerbeds. (Author's collection)

Figure 20: Fountain at Bourne Stream in January 1893
The pressure generated by a waterwheel kept the fountain working despite the ice.

Wishing-well shelter at Manly, Sydney
The shelter was provided for the Ukrainian sculptor to display his incredible work for the public; it remains as
a permanent memorial. (Courtesy of Manly Library Local Studies)

simple shelter would be desirable to allow the work to last for several months and
to enable several sand sculptures to be displayed in a single season, each one taking
some weeks to make. After various temporary structures, a more permanent one was
built. His income came from selling photographic postcards and charging admission.
The building changed to a wishing-well shelter after his temporary emigration.
Reportedly, three million coins were thrown over forty years to raise money for
a local hospital, a large model of which was in the shelter, together with pool and
rockery. Sadly, there was a vandalism problem and, later, the hospital model was 'lost'.
The shelter was refurbished in 2005 with painstakingly made aluminium panels
interpreting his life and work.

As well as sculpting in Melbourne, Brisbane and Santa Cruz, Suchomlin came to
Bournemouth on five occasions in the 1930s during the Australian winters. Although
much of his work reflected strong religious convictions, he also depicted famous
people of the day. Adolf Hitler was mocked as an Angel of Death but Amy Johnson
was celebrated. During the Great Depression, he made some political statements
with models of Rich Man Poor Man, Lap of Luxury and Pinch of Poverty. This last
model at Manly in 1931 showed a despondent family with three children around a
table, with only half a loaf of bread – it appears to be set in an attic and the father is
clearly jobless.

In 1936, Suchomlin was in Bournemouth and plying his trade on the famous
golden sands. The photograph includes the old King George V and the new King
Edward VIII in the artist's usual great detail – and what startling likenesses they are.
Indeed, they are so good that it is as well to state that there has been no enhancement

King George V and King Edward VIII modelled in sand, 1936
John Suchomlin's wonderful sculpture on Bournemouth sands in the year of abdication.

of the original photograph. It would be intriguing to know Suchomlin's opinion of the abdication crisis of that year and, for that matter, the alleged Nazi sympathies of the new king. However, as George V died in January 1936 and Edward VIII did not abdicate until December, the sculpture was doubtless made in the warmer weather, before the abdication storm had really broken. Had it done so earlier, this particular sand model might never have been crafted.

The artist kept returning to Australia to continue his work in the summer. It is thought that his most ambitious sculpture was created at Brisbane in 1959. Unfortunately, this superb model of the Last Supper, which took seventy days to make, was destroyed by vandals and he did not have the heart to rebuild it. His last known work was in 1962. Having finally retired, he suffered a stroke at his home north of Brisbane in 1973 and died the following year.

After making nearly 100 sand sculptures around the world, John Suchomlin left only the photographs as evidence. So it is that for a number of years before the Second World War the town hosted the work of a world-class sand modeller, a well-travelled and religious Ukrainian. We shall probably never know how and why he chose Bournemouth.

FIFTEEN

Albany

lbany (Fig. 13) is such an unusual apartment block that its story justifies inclusion in the book. Most residents of Bournemouth know it as a powerful landmark resembling a fortress, but perhaps few are aware of its history. It stands out as the most dominant feature of the skyline by far and defiantly challenges us all. Whilst many think it should never have been built, there are others, including some long-term residents, who absolutely love it. Around 1965, there was a rumour of Albany sliding into the sea! However, the general opinion at the time was that such gossip was far-fetched and simply mischievous – nearly fifty years later, the building remains in position and the general opinion vindicated.

Albany is Built

Having made probably the best Bournemouth property acquisition of all time under the 1805 Award, the Lord of the Manor, Sir George Ivison Tapps, owned the East Cliff and much else besides. His descendants have greatly enabled the town's development ever since on a leasehold basis, i.e. by retaining the freehold, the estate can grant a long ground lease and, when it expires, the property reverts to the estate. However, the consideration for these development deals is a far cry from the £5 per acre purchase price originally paid by Tapps. When a building is getting out of date and becoming more expensive to maintain, it can be at the end of its economic life. Moreover, this stage can often coincide with the expiration of a ninety-nine-year ground lease and the recovery by the estate of the land and buildings. At that point, it makes sense to look at redevelopment options and repeat the cycle. As we shall see later, leasehold enfranchisement can now prevent this traditional approach.

In 1961, however, before the days of enfranchisement, the traditional approach was used for the site of Albany. The estate had granted long ground leases on two sites in the nineteenth century, resulting in two large blocks of mansions being built, which had become dilapidated by that date. As the ground leases had expired, possession reverted to the estate as freeholders and a fresh 102-year lease was granted on the entirety to Langland Investments Ltd. As ground tenants, Langland contracted to demolish the existing buildings and erect 134 apartments and two maisonettes. One of the apartments has been divided into two to provide staff accommodation. The others vary between one, two, three and four-bedroom units, together with two penthouses. There is also an underground parking area for 107 cars. Although from some angles the scheme looks like a large white block, it is actually in the plan form of two 'Y's end to end and running parallel to the East Overcliff Drive. As its eighteen storeys make it the most prominent building on the East Cliff, it can be seen quite easily from both the Isle of Wight and the Isle of Purbeck.

It was certainly a prestigious scheme, with new flats selling at a price range from £4,600 to £25,000; the average was £8,300, a considerable figure at the time. The specification was high, including such features as 'entrance doors of solid wood veneered with Australian Walnut, polished window-boards and Twyfords close-coupled double-syphonic low-level WC suites'. The foyer area was designed by David Hicks, son-in-law of Lord Mountbatten. Yet sales began slowly, with only four disposed of by the end of 1963 and another eighteen in 1964. In 1967, one of the two penthouses sold, and all had found buyers by 1972.

Fighting the Elements

Bad weather is the enemy of sea-facing property in Bournemouth. In particular, strong prevailing winds and rain from the south-west do their best to penetrate a building's defences in exposed cliff-top locations; salty air is another detrimental factor. By 1967, there was water penetration of the external stonework, posing a risk to the structural steel frame. The remedy was to treat the affected areas by the coating of a bitumen seal. The ground tenants, Langland, agreed to be responsible for paying this cost for the entire building, on the basis of not seeking to recover it.

The next year, however, further works were required that did not seem to fall within this agreement, and occupiers had to pay. Water was getting through windows, affecting carpets and decorations. Charges of around £560,000 were made, and sinking fund money of around £105,000 was allocated for just two years. Over time, the repairs were completed and the building adequately secured against the elements. Nonetheless, it was an unwelcome, unexpected and heavy cost at the time, and must have given impetus to the determination shown later that all service charges must be clearly justified. Fig. 14 gives a fair idea of the sheer height and exposure of the building. Indeed, a second visit was needed to take the photograph because high winds restricted roof access on the first one.

Delights of Property Management

Running a block of flats is not an occupation that is everyone's cup of tea. Rather, it is a high-stress world of argument, endless telephone calls, unhappy tenants, letting and supervision of building works, and producing accounts. It may be that the development company's director, who held the head lease and managed Albany, was pleased to sell out to a resident, who in turn resold to another resident.

Thus it happened that a resident going back to 1968, and at one time chairwoman of the Albany Leaseholders' Association, decided to take the plunge – she purchased the head leasehold interest in 1982 from another resident in order to be able to manage Albany. Two years later she decided to refurbish the foyer, a project which included the encasement of the polished wooden pillars with white plaster, inset with niches containing ornaments. The chairman of the Association canvassed opinion, finding fifty-six against and only six in favour of the work; opposition was strong, especially as the Association had not been consulted. The head lessee disagreed. This could have been a breach of the terms of the head lease, but, when both parties wrote to the owners of the freehold, the estate declined to become involved. The matter died down and the plaster remains to this day. It was probably a case of opposition dying away as people got used to the change, especially as the head lessee had paid for the plastering of the pillars anyway.

As for the day-to-day running of Albany, the wealth of management detail goes beyond the scope of this chapter and a few examples must suffice: repair of hurricane damage in the big storm of 1987; foyer carpet replacement; fire detectors installed throughout; vertical blinds to foyer windows; relining roof-level water tanks; repainting southern elevation; twenty-four-hour porterage; maintenance of communal heating and hot-water system; internal telephone system; satellite TV and CCTV.

Court Injunction Against a Party

A splinter group which failed to get elected to the Albany Leaseholders' Association (ALA) committee went on to form a new group, the Albany Residents' Association (ARA). To celebrate its formation in 1993, they wanted to have an inaugural party in one of the flats, but were banned by the head lessee under threat of an injunction. As the ARA did not back down, the injunction was issued and the matter came to court. Although it was thrown out with costs against the head lessee plaintiff, an appeal followed and an interim hearing was next held. One argument was that the building was not strong enough to bear the weight of so many people in one flat. As the judge decided more structural evidence was needed, the matter was held over for a final hearing, which ran over two and a half days. There was good press and TV coverage of the case. The four defendants of the ARA were represented by a local solicitor, and the plaintiff by a London Queen's Counsel.

The final decision was to permit the inaugural party. Having considered the new structural evidence then available, the judge decided that there was, in fact, no risk to the structure. Costs mainly followed the action, with the defendants only being responsible for 25 per cent of their own costs; no costs were to be taken out of the service charge. The defendants had taken the big risk of being seriously out of pocket had they lost. By mid-1996 they got permission to hold the party, two and a half years after it was first announced.

On the night of the final judgement, a celebration party was held by the ARA and its supporters in one of the apartments. The ARA continued by organising regular parties, talks and outside concert visits. This socialising was a welcome and novel departure for the residents, who became more of a community.

Road to Buying the Freehold

Legislation has gradually moved towards protecting the interests of flat owners and occupiers. Service charges must now be properly broken down for tenants' information, and first refusal has to be given to associations of tenants if a landlord wants to sell his freehold interest. Such associations were also to be recognised by landlords and rent-assessment committees.

By 1992, the issue of leasehold reform was becoming of great interest. Once the unexpired term of a flat owner's lease falls below about sixty-five years, its value starts to be reduced. With that in prospect, the head lessee consulted with the freeholders and offered a twenty-five-year extension to flat owners at the existing ground rent for a price of £2,200. Although it sounded tempting, it meant prejudicing their interests because of legislation being planned – if that went through, the new law could be a better option. After a number of acrimonious letters were circulated, the offer was withdrawn.

In 1993, the new Act allowed ninety-year extensions or full enfranchisement, i.e. collective purchase by flat owners of the freehold. Both the ARA and ALA tried to get enough subscribers to pursue the Act but, at that time, neither group could achieve the two-thirds requirement. However, at the start of 2000, another lessee took an interest in obtaining enfranchisement and, together with interested committee members from the ALA, went on to unite the building. By August 2000, sufficient subscribers were found in order to create Albany Apartments Ltd, which worked to implement the 1993 Act and improve their terms of occupation. The head lessee's opposition had been withdrawn, newsletters were issued monthly and negotiations pursued. In March 2003, the freehold was finally acquired.

Enfranchisement party at Albany in 2003
Residents celebrate the move from feudal tenure to self-determination. (Courtesy of Peter Gayler)

A good illustration of the transfer of power and increase of freedom is the other party that was held after the 2003 enfranchisement. The foyer played host to a great champagne celebration – no need to get permission or any court decision for this event!

The Future

At the time of writing, Albany still has four original residents but, typically, ten apartments change hands every year. The water penetration issue is being tackled by annual maintenance to keep it under control. The building may be about fifty years old but it has not been allowed to deteriorate and should remain the most prominent cliff-top landmark for many years to come.

A major change has been the transfer of the freehold to Albany Apartments Ltd, which is owned by all the leaseholders, who in turn elect the directors of that company. Although there are managing agents, they are responsible to the directors, who are leaseholders themselves and naturally want to keep costs under control. Indeed, they are proud that they have never resorted to a special levy to cover maintenance costs since taking over in 2003. It is all as democratic as you can get. The community spirit is still encouraged by Albany Apartments Ltd, with regular parties and coffee mornings for the residents.

Harking back to the start of the story and the ancient landownership system then in place, Albany is a prime example of the modernisation of the law. In fifty years' time, there will be no reversion to the Lord of the Manor for redevelopment because the freehold will still be jointly owned by the residents. Acting as a true co-operative, it is they who decide on the future.

SIXTEEN

Longest Fireman's Pole

*I*n the 1990s, Bournemouth University acquired the town centre fire station, mainly for its Students' Union, and discovered an amazingly long fireman's pole. According to the Times Higher Education website, Bournemouth has the longest such pole in Britain at more than 14m. However, this feature, described as a 'campus curiosity', was not ideal for the students because it was no longer usable as designed – the holes in the floors had been blocked up!

After Bournemouth Central was replaced with a new building at the Wessex Way, Springbourne, it underwent a complete change; yet from the outside it still looks very much like a large town centre fire station. Its strategic location at No. 36 Holdenhurst Road was excellent, and indeed only a stone's throw from what is now Royal London House at the Lansdowne. These former insurance offices are now also occupied by the University. They were built on the site of the famous Metropole Hotel, which was destroyed by a Luftwaffe direct hit in 1943, causing a tragic loss of life. Following the purchase of Bournemouth Central by the university, it became known as the Old Fire Station, being an entertainment venue both for the public and for the Students' Union. Apparently, it even makes a 'profit' because the entry and bar charges, for events and drinks, help the Union's funds generally. The top floor is now given over to archive storage. All in all, it is difficult to imagine a bigger change of use.

The ground floor was mainly for the appliances, the first floor had canteen facilities and some officers' flats, the second floor included bedrooms and lockers, and the third floor had the usual recreation room (including snooker) to combat the occupational hazard of boredom. Despite callouts, some pretty drastic drills and good technical training, boredom is hard to eliminate altogether. At the highest level, access to the pole was through a self-closing metal gate which is still there. It is strange to reflect that the area, once used for recreation by firemen and many a dash for the pole, now houses some dry and dusty archives. That top floor is within the roof space, having an uninterrupted slope at the front and dormer windows to the rear. Fig. 15 shows the fireman's pole as now existing within a bar; it is of large diameter and of polished brass appearance. Whilst the great width is in order to give sufficient stability in use, the great length is in order to serve the full height of the building.

This was a large facility with four appliances, including one for special purposes and three for fire-fighting duties – there was a bay for each fire engine, whilst the right-hand bay was used for access to the rear. Film exists showing three appliances turning right into Holdenhurst Road at the same time. Emergency drills were most impressive, with a stopwatch being used to ensure a 'turnout for drill' within just sixty seconds.

But why was it such a high building in the first place? It seems that this building was planned to serve a considerable area from a built-up location. It therefore had to have sufficient accommodation to house the appliances and staff who worked the twelve-hour shifts. Without much land, the only way was up, and a very tall fire station was the consequence. Having placed the recreation area at third-floor level, the fire service's need for speed dictated the length of the pole – stairs would have been unacceptably slow.

Although some stations have staggered poles to reduce drop distances, this was evidently not considered essential here. Indeed, provided this extremely long pole was correctly used, there was little risk. Before using it, the practice was to look upwards to see that all was clear, and any fireman jumping on to it would shout 'on the pole' as a warning to the rest of the station. If this still sounds a little dangerous, perhaps the main thing is that no accidents are recalled. Nonetheless, there were health and safety arguments in favour of stairs in a 2006 three-storey Plymouth station, which was built without a pole. According to press reports at the time, such views were given short shrift by firemen who considered the pole method to be the quickest and safest way to do the job. However, the fire service now advises that there is no speed or safety problem in using the stairs.

Before leaving the main issue here of the lengthy pole, mention should be made of the competition: the West Midlands Fire Service claimed that Birmingham had

Central fire station, Holdenhurst Road
The former station is now occupied mainly by the Students' Union of Bournemouth University. (Author's collection)

the longest one in Europe at 40ft (12.2m). On investigation, it seems to have been at Lancaster Circus fire station, which no longer exists. Nonetheless, in the light of the claim, I have re-inspected the Old Fire Station to take the fireman's pole measurements, and can say that the Bournemouth version is 14.17m long from the ground floor to the ceiling of the third floor. As a minimum, another 0.15m must be assumed above that ceiling level for the top fixing, and possibly much more. Unfortunately, there was no access to establish the extra length that is out of sight. Applying, therefore, a total length of at least 14.32m, we find that it converts to 46.98ft, compared to a figure given of 47ft in a Bournemouth Fire Brigade video. Suffice it to say that it is a very long pole indeed and probably the longest in the country.

There are four 'extras' to mention. Firstly, did the pole ever get used 'unofficially'? It was possible to slide the pole with a cup of coffee in one hand and it was not unknown to travel it upside down. However, the story about a fireman sliding down head first with a complete tray of coffee is believed to be an exaggeration!

Secondly, what is the reason for towers at fire stations? They were initially to allow the canvas hoses to dry. After use, they would be scrubbed clean, tested to ensure there were no leaks, repaired if necessary and then hung vertically to dry with the aid of a top-level pulley system. In the present days of plastic hoses, there is no need for a vertical drying system. Another use, which is still vital today, concerns safety training with ladders. Firemen regularly practise simulated rescues using ladders placed against the tower at various angles and heights.

The third 'extra' concerns Omo the cat at the old Pokesdown fire station, which closed in the 1970s. The cat's owner was the fire officer who lived in the residential quarters above the appliance area. Being completely white (hence the name) and totally deaf, it was well known at the station that the cat was not permitted to venture out of the quarters under any circumstances. Yet one day, in the early 1960s, Omo was spotted crossing the very busy road at the junction of Seabourne Road and Christchurch Road. The horrified firemen immediately had the lights turned red for all traffic directions, a procedure normally used to allow a clear run for a fire appliance in an emergency. To the great puzzlement of the watching public, no fire engine appeared. Instead, the officers rushed out in force to catch and return Omo, who was none the worse for the adventure.

The final tale concerns a ghost. Standing rules have always been that firemen awaiting a call need to be dressed but do not need to have footwear. That way, they can go straight to the appliance and pull on their boots en route. The exception is the driver who needs shoes to drive and would place them next to his bunk in the night. New recruits were told that a driver's shoes were often moved by the Bournemouth Central ghost to a different place from where he had left them at his bedside. Once new officers realised that the shoes were actually moved by a colleague, they would happily join the scam for the benefit of the next recruits.

SEVENTEEN

Mayor Whitelegg and Some Recollections

*I*t would be a mistake to imagine that being a councillor and Mayor of Bournemouth is all dull duties and bureaucracy. Whilst it is true that there are endless committees to attend and policies to decide, there seems to be some fun along the way.

Philip Whitelegg, born in Sale, Cheshire in 1917, has kindly contributed examples of the unexpected. As he has been in the town since 1937, and was a councillor for Redhill Park Ward for fifty years from 1953, there has been immense experience upon which to draw, and space only permits a few anecdotes. When he was Mayor in 1966/1967, there was a lot going on and a tightly packed timetable of events. Moreover, in

Philip Whitelegg

the interests of good relations with nearby authorities, he encouraged what might be termed 'mayoral co-operation'. As a result, he jointly attended some evening events with the Mayors of Poole and Christchurch – indeed, the press dubbed them the 'three night mayors'! July 1966 saw the first official visit of a reigning monarch to the town, and Mayor Whitelegg duly welcomed the Queen and the Duke of Edinburgh. It was a crowded, flag-waving and highly successful occasion.

Perhaps the level of responsibility means that some lighter moments are essential to the work of mayors and councillors. The stories begin with a recalcitrant, yet increasingly embarrassed, Pavilion manager and his appointment with the Mayor. A toe-curling image is conjured up of the manager's growing awareness of the repeated arrival of the mayoral limousine, relentlessly travelling around the block and back to the main entrance by the fountain.

This first account concerns Alderman Harry Mears, Mayor of Bournemouth in 1953, 1963 and 1964. He demanded that protocol be exercised towards the Mayor of the Borough, especially by officials of the council. Upon one of his first visits as Mayor, to the Pavilion in Bournemouth, the general manager of the building was not present to receive him or the Mayoress. The Mayor directed the chauffeur, Reg, to 'drive on' and make a circuit, calling again after a few minutes in the hope that the manager would be on the steps to receive. Unfortunately, upon arriving a second time, there was still no manager. So the Mayor told the chauffeur to go round the circuit once again; this performance took place at least two more times until the manager at last appeared, very 'hot under the collar', and of course very apologetic. The Mayor, one can easily understand, was not slow to display his anger and disappointment at being kept waiting.

Another case concerns the Mayor of Poole. He was visiting a naval frigate and, in the navy's tradition of offering hospitality to visitors – especially visitors of importance – there were ample 'refreshments' available to the Mayor and his entourage. However, the time to say goodbye inevitably arrived but the Mayor was somewhat reluctant to take his leave, and enjoyed his last drink with gusto. The captain became impatient at the delay shown by his guests and requested again that the party went ashore. But unfortunately these pleas were ignored. The captain issued one last request for the party's departure within a short time limit. Still this had no effect and so the captain gave orders to 'cast off' with the party still aboard. The party, with the exception of the Mayor, left the ship via the gangway. When the ship began to slowly move away from the landing stage, the Mayor realised he would become a reluctant member of the crew. He immediately made his way to the opening on the deck where the gangway had been attached and took a flying leap across the gap which was rapidly widening between the ship and the landing stage, and just made it without any aftereffects.

The next story, concerning the double meaning of words spoken without deep thought, is about Councillor Bill Wareham, who wished to intervene in a council debate, the subject being the Northbourne Sewerage Works. An argument was being conducted by several councillors when Bill jumped up and spoke forcibly to the Mayor: 'Mr Mayor, I wish to jump into this.'

Sometimes feigned ignorance produces a laugh, like the occasion when a Labour stalwart, Councillor Arthur Iggulden, asked the chairman of the Beach & Pavilion Committee: 'Can the chairman tell the council what is candyfloss?' The chairman, Alderman Alfred Little, said, 'Well to put it into a nut-shell it's a mouthful of nothing.' The councillor then very quickly said, 'Oh, we get mouthfuls of that here, don't we Mr Mayor?' ('Here' was of course the council chamber.)

In his capacity as Mayor, Philip attended many conferences which he opened on behalf of the borough. One such conference was the Retail & Trade Electrical Association and, having opened the proceedings, he was followed by Gerald Nabarro (chairman of the Association), who was a well-known MP with a penchant for an expansive style of speaking. In his speech, Mr Nabarro boasted his strong support of many electrical appliances, saying, 'I am of course a strong advocate of the use of electricity in the house and elsewhere. I use an electric razor, an electric toothbrush, an electric kettle, an electric coffee percolator, an electric iron and of course an electric fire.' Whereupon a voice loudly shouted, 'What about an electric chair?' Without a pause, Nabarro replied, his face wreathed in smiles, 'Oh, I'm getting Harold Wilson [Labour Prime Minister at that time] to occupy that!'

The last anecdote concerns a keen chapel-attending lady councillor with a Welsh background, who was not completely *au fait* with modern life and the change which took place in customs, language, etc. over the years. The council decided in this particular year to allow the pierhead shops to open fronting the promenade, and also allowed the ice-cream kiosks to open on Sundays during the season. This regulation would undoubtedly attract many more people, young and old, including those of the teenage category to be seen on the prom. The good lady was against Sunday openings, and at the council meeting exclaimed to the members: 'I'm against this relaxation of the rules. You don't know what it may lead to – on occasions, I've been solicited whilst walking along the promenade.'

Thanks are due to Philip Whitelegg for these insights; at least we can rest assured that our elected members are human beings with a proper sense of humour!

EIGHTEEN

Faltering Start but a High-Speed Finish

hy has Bournemouth been one of the fastest 'growth towns' in the country? And why was it slow to take off? From a hesitant beginning, it became an enormous success and created a superb reward for those benefiting from the land allocations under the Christchurch Inclosure Act of 1802. Was the Act promoted by local landowners just to gain the value of new pine plantations or was it all about development potential? This chapter looks at the slow start and the remarkably flexible and triumphant nature of the later expansion.

Early Development

The 1805 Award changed how the newly enclosed land was held: land subject to commons rights became freehold land with vacant possession. This permitted the new freeholder to improve it or build on it. The Lord of the Manor had a sort of tenure of commons land under his 'lordship' but was prevented from improving it by commons rights such as turbary, i.e. the right to cut turf for fuel. By its creation of proper freehold interests, the Award thus enabled improvement and development of that land previously used in common by the residents of the various tythings.

As any developer knows, it is essential to build for genuine future occupiers having money to rent or buy; otherwise, one is on the road to a white elephant and bankruptcy. Certainly, there were plenty of enclosures made elsewhere permitting new building, but they did not become swiftly growing towns. Hence the growth question remains – why so fast at Bournemouth and why the initial delay? The short answer must relate to a timely mixture of local enterprise and the special attributes of the land. It is no accident that the establishment of a big town coincided with a combination of forces: national prosperity, the growing popularity of watering places and the great Bournemouth selling points. It would be a big mistake to underestimate them – the warm climate, the beaches, the claimed health benefits of the pine trees and the beautiful setting.

Just a few properties were built by Lewis Tregonwell (chiefly for family and friends) after his land purchase in 1810, but there was little activity otherwise for twenty-five years. Although he planted some trees and let cottages for sea-bathing holidays, it was all rather slow and minimal. Perhaps he and his wife wanted it that way. If so, who could blame them? The Drax Grosvenors occupied Cliff Cottage on the other side of the road from the founder's house, so adding to the social scene of the tiny village. The founder's main site of 36 acres ran from Exeter Lane by the meadow adjacent to the Bourne Stream to just past the present Tregonwell Road on the west. The northern boundary ran along Commercial Road to the Square (excluding the site of Debenhams and some nearby land), and the southern one ran parallel to Priory Road, excluding most of the BIC site but including the Punshon Memorial Church site. The illustration of the 1835 map gives an idea of how little had been done since the first land purchase twenty-five years earlier. But the 1851 map shows considerable acceleration.

Map of Bourne in 1835
(Courtesy of Bournemouth Libraries and Ordnance Survey, © Crown copyright)

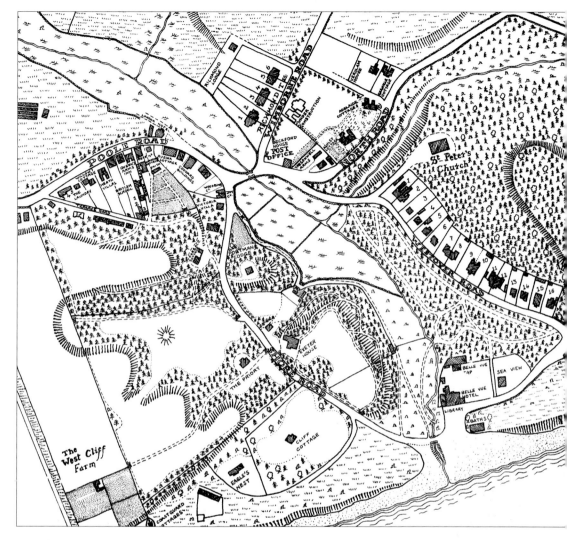

Map of Bourne in 1851
(Courtesy of Bournemouth Libraries and Ordnance Survey, © Crown copyright)

Lewis died in 1832 and Henrietta in 1846. The estate was then inherited by their son John, who proceeded to encourage development. His mother had become difficult in her later years and was against business use. But eventually, John's efforts paid off – fourteen years after his first attempt to let the land, building began in Cranborne Road with a ninety-eight-year ground lease from 1860 at £15 per annum. Similarly, an 1848 attempt to lease 23 acres failed, and it was not until 1864 that land at Exeter Park was ground leased for ninety-nine years for £130 per annum. Having gained hugely under the 1805 Award and sold some land near the Brook, the Lord of the Manor, Sir George Ivison Tapps, appeared to be resisting development of his own land. He established some pine plantations, but did little more before his death in 1835. Nonetheless, his work in starting the town was important for three reasons: obtaining more prime acres of freehold property than anyone else, selling land to the founder, and setting the scene for a health resort by planting enormous numbers of pines.

In summary, at the same time that the well-off were flocking for their health to various spa towns around the country – such as Bath, Malvern and Hove – the speed of Bournemouth's growth was slow from 1810 to 1835. The nearest possible spa was at the still undeveloped Boscombe, but the health resort potential of what is now the town centre certainly went on to prove itself over the next twenty-five years. The lack of a spa facility was more than counteracted by the big Bournemouth selling points, which competing spa towns simply did not have. The conclusion is that the faltering start was simply due to the lack of a strong driving force at that time. Nobody was yet sure enough of the likely demand to start building on a large scale. In addition, both Tapps and Mrs Tregonwell preferred the status quo.

Expansion Gathers Pace

A turning point was the inheritance of the Manor in 1835 by Tapps' son, Sir George Tapps-Gervis, a man uniquely placed to carry it all forward. He thought the time was right to make a health resort and gave a big impetus to the embryo town by encouraging building. Was it something of a gamble? Why should it work now? Well, the times were changing and the attractions of the town were coming into their own. The Award had provided properly for ownership and control of the land and adequate major roads. In addition, the trail-blazing scheme known as Bourne Tregonwell had succeeded and would expand after the death of Mrs Tregonwell.

The main thing about getting ownership of a large tract of land is that it could cost very little but might later create its own very high value, and this is exactly what has happened in Bournemouth. In 1802, the present-day Square had virtually no buildings, and Poole was connected to Christchurch merely by tracks over what was called Pool Heath. Who wants to have low-quality desolate land suitable for trees, being generally inadequate for arable and even pasture use? But today, it is that very same land which is 'so urban' that sustains a series of multi-million-pound property deals – its development has created its own value.

The natural advantage of arguably the best seaside setting in the country was soon aided by the skilful management of the town's growth. Sir George Tapps-Gervis was enthusiastic during his six years of pro-active estate management until his death in 1842. Lots of plans were drawn up by the brilliant Christchurch architect Benjamin Ferrey, carefully scrutinised and partially implemented. Financial risks to the estate were minimised by the ground rent system whereby long leases were granted at low rents and all the development risk was carried by tenants who erected their own premises. Money was soon being made. He made available the Westover Road land for villas and the site at the end for a hotel, now the Royal Bath. After his death, trustees were employed to carry on the good work, as his son was still a child. Decimus Burton replaced Ferrey in the role of promoting new development.

One Ferrey scheme for concentric circles of houses on the East Cliff was criticised by the health-resort expert, Dr Granville, who visited by invitation in 1841, and it was never built. No matter; the important thing was that the small village of Bournemouth was open for business and had some big ideas. Indeed, the celebrated Dr Granville gave his vital endorsement of the town as becoming the best watering place in

Scheme by Benjamin Ferrey (1810–1880) in 1836
Although his Pleasure Gardens pagoda opposite the pier was not built, the Bath Hotel and the Westover
Road villas were developed as shown. (Courtesy of Bournemouth Libraries)

the country. He also recommended that pleasure gardens be made from the rough
meadow between the sea and what is now the Square. It was done, as was his idea for
a church to be built at the same level as the houses to encourage attendance by the
convalescents. His strategic direction of 1841 was most timely and effective.

Enormous expansion took place between 1835 and 1861. The Bournemouth
Commissioners were established in 1856 and gave a fresh boost. Their initial boundary
was very odd – a circular line drawn at a 1-mile radius from the front door of the Belle
Vue Hotel, which was always called 'the boarding house', on a site now occupied by
the Pavilion. By 1861, the population was 1,707 in respect of the Commissioners' area
of 1.8 square miles. The census gave 5,896 by 1871. However, census figures should
be used with caution because of boundary extensions. By 1881, the town area had
increased to 2.6 square miles but the population by nearly three times to 16,859. By
1901, the town had achieved County Borough status in respect of 9.1 square miles and
the census gave 59,762. Ten years later the same land area supported a population of
78,764. We can clearly say that it was a high-speed finish.

We have seen how it took forty-six years from Henrietta Tregonwell visiting Bourne
Chine to the village of Bournemouth securing the Bournemouth Improvement Act in
1856. Despite the controversies and economic problems which lay ahead, the faltering
stage was well and truly over. In 1860, the eminent Dr Spencer Thomson claimed that
Bournemouth was now known as the Winter Garden of England. Let us now turn to
the successful way in which Bournemouth expanded by embracing and adapting to
change over time.

The first development phase, after Granville's guidance of 1841, was mainly as a
select health resort for the well-off in need of recuperation. Later, the same features
of location, golden sands, warm climate and the inevitable scented pines were used
to sell the second phase as a unique seaside resort. Hence, when it was felt in the
First World War that there were simply too many bath chairs for the good of the

town, the name of Invalids' Walk was changed to Pine Walk and its 'resort status' was marketed much more than its 'health status'. Once the initial development began in earnest, its sheer speed meant that few of the early buildings have survived. Although the Commissioners insisted on wide, curving roads and a most spacious general layout, this was all part of the strictly commercial culture of the town, one that persists to this day. To be a success, Bournemouth had to be 'special'.

Having managed to combine the 'bath-chair and National Sanatorium' image with upmarket holiday-making, the town gained further from the new rail links – although for some, this was an adaptation too far. Here we have a classic Bournemouth compromise: the new railway was eventually accepted as necessary to promote the town, but it had to be specially built, where possible, in cuttings and well away from the centre. The trains were needed to help the town's businesses but the 'quality difference' compared to everywhere else had to be maintained by tucking the railways out of sight. Day trippers came back for a fortnight by the sea, a lot of small hotels were needed, and the building industry went from strength to strength, as did all the ancillaries such as shops, pubs and cinemas. To the chagrin of some, the resort's fashionably upmarket days were over. Yet the culture of quality remained, so that when the trams arrived even they had to be built to 'Bournemouth standard' – it had to be a better destination for the discriminating visitor than any other resort in the country.

By the 1960s, many visitors with fond memories of the town wanted to retire to Bournemouth, but there were simply not enough flats and bungalows. Not many could afford an expensive detached property in say, Boscombe Manor, nor did they wish to settle in the less attractive parts of town. Some bungalow estates were built, but the biggest change was the demolition of the large old houses in big plots to erect multi-storey blocks of flats, a process that continues to this day. It is also not surprising that a town so wedded to private enterprise has made sure that the popular grammar schools, and their big contribution to social mobility, have survived. In more recent years, the same thinking has continued with the enlarged university and attraction of national headquarters, conferences and language schools.

Certainly since the 1850s, therefore, there has been a sustained thrust by landowners, entrepreneurs and local government to achieve a fast and profitable enhancement of Bournemouth by capitalising on its unique setting and natural advantages. Although the very select nature of the town had been cultivated in its early days, that policy was driven by economics. It is the very same economics that has driven later, and some feel undesirable, changes – recent examples would be the enormous club scene and the Boscombe surf reef. It is easy to imagine the Commissioners debating how to move their business interests forward together with those of the town: 'Let us capitalise on our natural advantages and make Bournemouth the most attractive destination in the country for the wealthy in need of recuperation.' In later years, councillors might say: 'We must move with the times and secure a good slice of the holiday market even if that means more crowds and some loss to our "select" image.'

Here is a town which has always believed in adapting to a changing world and prospering along the way. Whilst its future success may prove more difficult to achieve now that there is little land left, history tells us that Bournemouth will probably think of something!

NINETEEN

Remedies at a Watering Place

ournemouth was identified early in its development as probably the best 'watering place' in the country. The expression implies a seaside resort often with mineral or spring water and likely to have good bathing facilities. The planting of an enormous number of pine trees converted the heath into resin-scented woodland, which was deemed by most doctors (including the Queen's physician) to be most beneficial to the health. On the other hand, doctors now say that pine scent has no place in treating chest conditions and interestingly, turpentine oil is only an inactive ingredient in Vicks VapoRub.

When the town was originally promoted for the better-off element of society and those amongst them in need of convalescence, many came here to use the Royal National Sanatorium, which opened in 1855. At that time, the remarketing of the town as a resort for all classes had yet to start. Medical knowledge being much less advanced in the nineteenth century, people tended to believe in unproven remedies. The town's newspapers were regularly carrying adverts which appear to be especially designed to appeal to the desperate and the hypochondriac. Certainly, suppliers of these 'cures' felt that promotion in Bournemouth was commercially viable – possibly more so than elsewhere.

The *Bournemouth Observer and Fashionable Visitors' List* carried these pieces in various issues in 1875:

Valuable Discovery for the Hair
 – If your hair is turning grey or white, or falling off, use 'the Mexican Hair Renewer', for it *will positively restore in every case Grey or White hair* to its original colour, without leaving the disagreeable smell of most 'Restorers'. It makes the hair charmingly beautiful, as well as promoting the growth of the hair on bald spots, where the glands are not decayed. Certificate from Dr Versmann on every bottle, with full particulars. Ask your Chemist for 'THE MEXICAN HAIR RENEWER', prepared by HENRY C. GALLUP, 493 Oxford-street, London, and sold by Chemists and Perfumers everywhere at 3s. 6d. per bottle.

'For The Blood Is The Life'
 – See Deuteronomy, chap.xii, verse 23.

CLARKE'S WORLD FAMED BLOOD MIXTURE
THE GREAT BLOOD PURIFIER & RESTORER
SKIN DISEASES, Eruptions, Blotches, Ulcerated Sore Legs, Glandular Swellings, Cancerous Ulcers, Spots, Pimples, Pustules, Boils, Carbuncles, Ringworms, Scald Heads, Sore Eyes, Erysipelas, Itch, Scurf, Discolorations of the Skin, Humours and Diseases of the Skin of whatever name or nature, are literally carried out of the systems in a short time by the use of this world-famed Medicine.

IMPORTANT ADVICE TO ALL. – Cleanse the vitiated blood whenever you find its impurities bursting through the skin in pimples, eruptions or sores; cleanse it when you find it obstructed and sluggish in the veins, cleanse it when it is foul, and your feelings will tell you when. Keep the blood pure and the health of the system will follow.

The Bible reference in Deuteronomy (above) actually bans the eating of blood: 'Only be sure that thou eat not the blood; for the blood *is* the life; and thou mayest not eat the life with the flesh.' F.J. Clarke was a Lincoln chemist who supplied the mixture throughout the UK and the world. In the same way as for the Mexican Hair Renewer, a reassuring blue glass was used for the bottle. It was still possible to buy this product, albeit with different ingredients, as recently as 1968. According to the Quack Doctor website, original ingredients of the Blood Mixture were: water coloured by burnt sugar, with a small amount of potassium iodide, sal volatile, chloroform and syrup sweetener. An empty antique blue bottle sold on eBay in June 2011 for 99p.

Mont Dore Hotel
When built in 1885, this luxurious hotel was regarded as the finest building in Bournemouth.

Mont Dore Hotel

On a more serious note, this high-class hotel (destined to become the Town Hall in 1921) was described as the finest building in town when it opened its doors to invalids, residents and visitors in 1885. Set amidst pines upon an eminence in 4 acres of the town centre, the hotel was claimed to have the most varied and perfect system of baths in the kingdom. These included Turkish, douche, needle, plunge, pine, seawater 'pumped up from the ocean', medicated and others. Altogether, there were twenty modes of using water externally. The bathing part of the premises was connected by a glass corridor to the hotel proper. Water was even imported from the springs in Auvergne, thereby giving exactly the same facility as the famous Auvergne Baths – indeed, a town guide explains that those baths were the design model for the Mont Dore Hotel. However, due to the mild climate in Bournemouth, the baths continued throughout the year, instead of just June to September as in France.

Treatments were available for gout, rheumatism and the respiratory organs. Patients could have inhalation, vapour, throat and nasal irrigations. Catering for up to 200 visitors, the imposing building had many facilities, including five tennis courts. Reading the town guides, one was led to realise that it was on the best site, truly palatial in nature, and notable for excellent food and wine.

Whether ailments were real or imagined, Victorian Bournemouth could certainly satisfy the needs of those wanting treatment according to their means.

TWENTY

Of Plank, Smuggling-Outrage and Chapel

*I*f you stand at the Square today, it is a scene of dense urban development except for the Pleasure Gardens. There are shops, crowds and all the activities of a busy town centre. Yet a map of 1790 shows a scene that was as different as could possibly be imagined – it was a desolate place, having just one small building and where only a plank was deemed necessary to cross the Brook, now called the Bourne Stream. The turnpike road from Christchurch ran over the heath, crossed the Brook as a ford and climbed up Poole Hill.

The town centre has been developed in a shallow chine, whilst the Lower Pleasure Gardens used to be a rather swampy meadow that was regularly inundated by the sea. North of the road crossing over the Brook was Decoy Pond, which was created to attract ducks for netting. Later, there were shooting parties of wildfowlers. This is not the same location as today's Coy Pond, which is much further upstream. However, even in 1790 a track did follow the line of Exeter Road from the shore to the turnpike road. A smuggler could take that track to a building called Decoypond House (site of the present Debenhams) as a stopping-off point. He might then branch off the turnpike road and maintain direction along Decoy Pond Lane by the west side of the Brook.

What is known about Decoypond House? It has been otherwise identified in various places as Decoy Cottage, Bourne Cottage, Bourn House and a pair of semis: Decoy Cottage and Bourne House. Despite some uncertainty here about naming, it is generally agreed to have been the haunt of wildfowlers and smugglers. One theory is that it was a single farmhouse with a changing name occupied by a man with several jobs – stockman for the meadows (now the Pleasure Gardens), gamekeeper for the Decoy Pond, smuggler and inn-keeper.

By 1838, the big sixteen-villa Westover Road scheme was being promoted by Sir George Tapps-Gervis, and he was anxious for a place of worship to serve the growing community. That year, he converted this building into a chapel, as shown on the sketch. Compared to the sketch on the 1790 map, it can be seen that windows were provided with arches, and a bell tower erected. On Sundays there were two Church of England services, and during the week it was a schoolroom. E. W. Leachman (*see* Bibliography) described the building as formerly being two cottages. He says: 'The upstair rooms of one cottage were left as a gallery for musicians!' Hence we might envisage the present Square as virgin land in 1790, except for this one building.

And what of the stories which claim it was a smugglers' haunt? Were they true or merely another myth? We might not know who built it or occupied it, but a horrifying report in the *Salisbury & Wiltshire Journal* of 20 December 1762 provides solid evidence about its use. An official notice was placed by the Custom House, London, offering £50 rewards upon conviction for apprehension of members of a 'gang of supposed Smugglers'. Claiming to be a King's Press Gang, they had performed an outrage against Joseph Manuel, a boy of sixteen. Having forced open the door of his father's house in Iford at 8 p.m. on 1 September 1762, they violently seized the lad and 'forced him down to Bourn-Mouth to a lonely House there, called the Decoypond House, notoriously frequented by smugglers …' After detention there, the boy was put in a boat, later thrown into the sea and then carried on board 'the Smuggling Cutter, the *Ranger Privateer*' to Alderney. He was treated with great cruelty and would probably have been murdered if 'some few of the crew, relenting, had not interposed'. He was compelled to fire off an over-charged blunderbuss 'with intent it is supposed to destroy him' – it burst and tore off his left thumb. Joseph managed to escape and get home. The outrage was believed to have been ordered by some principal smugglers of the coast as a reprisal for him giving information to the revenue men.

Reverting to the Brook, a walker travelling east or west could cross by the plank, which had a ford alongside for horses, carts and carriages. The Bourne Plank was followed by a pedestrian rustic bridge over the stream. According to Pascoe Marshall's

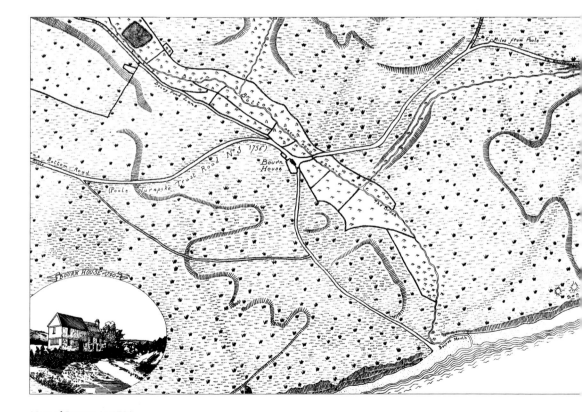

Map of Bourne in 1790
A desolate spot crossed by the Christchurch to Poole road and having no known buildings except Bourn House. (Courtesy of Bournemouth Libraries and Ordnance Survey, © Crown copyright)

Bournemouth's first place of worship, 1838
Two semi-detached cottages, probably Bourn House and Decoy Cottage, were converted to a chapel and schoolroom. Residents of Bourne village attended for Church of England services. (Sketch by J.M. Elwes)

reminiscences (*see* Bibliography), it was not until 1849 that the road was shaped and the footbridge built at a cost of £100. He confirms the mapping evidence by saying that the stream ran open across the road and vehicles had to go through it, whilst pedestrians used the bridge. At that time this area was known as the Bridge not the Square, which is a name of uncertain origin.

Kathleen Chilver (*see* Bibliography) has researched some old records from Holdenhurst. In 1722, Holdenhurst's Poor Rate records the expense of financing the repair of both the road at 'Boorne' and the plank bridge. In 1735, the road at 'Bourn' cost the Overseers of the Poor £1 10*s*. In 1743, the repair cost of 'Boorne Plank' was £1 4*s*, and in 1763 it was £1 3*s* 1*d* – this last time restored by Joseph Troke. By the time photography became common, the plank and the later rustic footbridge had been replaced by a road bridge above a culvert. For example, a photograph from the Day Collection (*c.* 1865) shows a stone bridge suitable for carriages. In the eighteenth century, it was clearly deemed essential for a good plank to be provided and maintained on the rates to avoid those on foot having to splash through the Brook.

Could people in 1790 visualise the Square of twenty-first-century Bournemouth? Perhaps the 2007 shot from the Bournemouth Eye (Fig.16) answers the question.

TWENTY-ONE

Astonishing Drainage System

Sewage disposal in Bournemouth has always been rather innovative. For example, the first outfalls into Poole Bay were more satisfactory than in most coastal towns simply because they were longer. It was good forward-thinking for the time. These first two outfalls near to Bournemouth Pier are now used for storm or emergency purposes only, but their lengths are considerable at 806m and 587m. Today, water quality at the beaches is very good. The amazing Coastal Interceptor Sewer has achieved a great result by reversing the direction of flow for most of the sewage – instead of going south to the sea it goes north for treatment and the river. Few realise that all of the foul drainage and much of the storm drainage systems discharge to the Stour after passing through Holdenhurst and Kinson sewage treatment works. Excess storm water passes to Poole Bay or the river Stour, after 6mm screening. Flows entering the Stour eventually reach the sea via the Run by Mudeford Quay.

No longer do residents and tourists have to run the regular risk of encountering raw sewage whilst swimming in the sea. In view of the fast expansion of the town and its differences in levels, this is no mean achievement. Equally, there is little or no sign of any adverse content in the river and harbour. Occasionally, a small amount of brown foam or scum is visible in the harbour, but this is usually algae and not output from the sewage works. Indeed, the water company uses ultraviolet light for its disinfection process at river outfalls – a process that is above the normal industry standard. But there will always be challenges, such as the recent Wessex Way odour complaints. Those have been addressed by a scheme for the replacement of inlet works, a task that was also required because that part of the installation is at the end of its life. But as a company spokesman was careful to point out, sewage treatment works will never be odour-free by their very nature.

Whilst the great majority of the current Bournemouth system is separated, i.e. the surface water and foul drainage runs in different pipes, the town centre was at one time served by a combined network. After the very early self-draining gravel roads were upgraded to hard surfaces (requiring their own road drains) and the time came to have public sewers for individual properties, those same pipes were also used for foul drainage. Separation has been introduced increasingly since the 1930s. Today, most of the town centre is not combined – indeed, some of the surface water from Old Christchurch Road feeds into the Bourne Stream at a point hidden by a weir. As for the considerable surface water run-off from hard surfaces like roofs, much of it does not enter the public system at all, being sent instead to soakaways at individual properties.

Yet despite the general separation in the town, during storms a significant amount of storm water is contained in the sewer flows going to Holdenhurst and Kinson. This is a desirable outcome in a way, because a town's surface water is not exactly clean – it contains road dirt, animal droppings, vehicle exhaust residues and tree pollen. That water is greatly purified before discharge into the river Stour. Would the ideal world have total separation, with surface water going directly to the sea and foul water directly to the works? Possibly, but that would be highly expensive to change now. The works would be much smaller and less expensive to build and run, whilst there would be no foul material in the sea or on land at time of flood due to extreme weather. But even at the time of the decision to build the Coastal Interceptor Sewer, such a change is not likely to have been financially feasible. In any case, there may be regulation in the future to clean up surface water discharges and, if so, Bournemouth may be well-placed with its current system.

In the early days, after the decision was taken to replace the individual cesspools and septic tanks for each property, the three initial drainage areas were the town centre, Westbourne and Boscombe. The first took waste from the Bourne Valley to a point near to the pier, where a macerator station broke it up and pumped it through the outfalls. The second discharged at Alum Chine and Boscombe, and was drained by gravity – again, its macerator also created liquefied slurry that was taken well out into the bay. Compared to raw sewage, the much finer material broke down biologically more quickly.

More outfalls followed at Fisherman's Walk and Hengistbury Head, but not all with macerators. This sometimes caused problems with inshore drift during the tourist season. As a child swimming at Southbourne in the 1950s, I can well remember sometimes 'going through the motions' as we used to say! The large development of the Winton area created a pressing need for its own solution, as provided by 1920 – a drain along Queen's Park Avenue, through Littledown, Tuckton, Broadway and out at Hengistbury Head. Later, the Northern Main was introduced to cater for further town expansion. This ran along Castle Lane to a pumping station at Iford, where it joined the Winton sewage at Tuckton before proceeding to the Hengistbury outfall.

It was realised as early as the 1930s that there was a need for improvement in order to assist the tourist industry or the 'holiday image' of the town. After some planning for a new joint drainage authority to create a unified system serving Bournemouth, Poole and Christchurch, the Second World War arrived to halt the discussions. In the event, Bournemouth decided to go it alone in the 1950s, resulting in the excitingly innovative Holdenhurst scheme and its air-pumping design, quaintly known as the 'activated sludge process'. By forcing streams of air upwards through the large rectangular open-topped holding tanks, the usual speed of biological action was greatly increased. Although it used more energy, the sewage works could be much smaller.

Yet planning was soon needed for a phased expansion, as further areas of the town's drainage were connected into the plant (initially it was only serving Winton). A major extension was also constructed during the 1990s, including additional storm treatment capacity. The extraordinary drainage revolution had begun. No longer was the town's sewage to be pumped out to sea at some risk to the beaches. The new plan was to treat it and take out the residual harmless water by the natural flow of the river Stour.

We have almost reached the point of discussing the magic of the Coastal Interceptor Sewer (CIS). The town's need for pollution-free seawater was not easy to fulfil. How was everything to be drained from the town (with its differences in level, not least due to the chines) and also biologically treated, when it had always gone to the sea? In answer, enormous new tunnels were hand-dug through the sandy subsoil to create concrete-lined, circular cross-section drains of 6ft internal diameter. Broadly, the CIS runs from the east and from the west near to the cliffs, meets at Boscombe and then flows by gravity to the Holdenhurst Sewage Works by the river Stour. Along the way, it intercepts the existing south-flowing drains, obviating any need to pollute Poole Bay.

It is helpful to keep in mind the topography of the town when looking at the sea outfall method. Bournemouth is on a plateau that falls away at different gradients on all sides. The main cliffs are about 100ft high but are cut through by chines, which have inevitably affected drainage plans over the years. For example, the drainage area at Kinson has its own works near to the river Stour, whilst Westbourne was logically drained to the Alum Chine outfall. On the other side, the eastern part of Southbourne shelves and naturally drains towards Hengistbury Head. In between, some newer southern parts of town, such as Boscombe and Fisherman's Walk, soon required southern outfalls. In these two cases, any attempt to connect to the pre-existing network would have caused overload. Sewage disposal upgrade plans were essential. In the same fashion that land falls to Hengistbury and the east, it also falls to the north and the river; it is this key factor that allowed the CIS scheme to operate. Without that slope down to the north, it could not have been done.

Let us now look at how the present extraordinary installation actually works. It was not necessary to make changes to the incline of the general drains of the town because the CIS design allowed them still to operate by gravity from north to south – a good thing too because otherwise the costs of digging up the roads etc. would have been prohibitive. The upgrade has been called the Coastal Interceptor Sewer because it intercepts the south-flowing drains. Moreover, as a result of the sandy subsoil and the ability to place it where required, deeply underground, most of the CIS itself is gravitational with only a minority of the tunnels taking sewage which has first been pumped uphill.

The first connection to the new works at Holdenhurst was directly from Winton through a large double pipe. It ran from a point close to Shaft One (i.e. one of the highly accessible junctions of main sewers located just to the south of the Cooper Dean roundabout, where Castle Lane meets the Wessex Way). This shaft, which has a triple pipe connection to the works, is at the lowest point of the tunnels system. For instance, there is a tunnel running downhill from Sea Road, Boscombe to Woodland Walk (Shaft Four) and from there downhill to Shaft One. So far, we have seen that there are two connections to the works, one for the Winton sewage and one for the majority of the town's sewage via Shaft One. There is a third direct one from the west for the area north of Castle Lane.

Bournemouth Pier Approach still receives its normal amount of foul and surface water from the Bourne Valley. But in addition, the West Cliff part of the CIS directs much more there, having intercepted the material that used to flow out to sea at Alum Chine. However, it is all now pumped uphill to a point just above the Royal Bath Hotel, whence it is taken by gravity to Woodland Walk, Boscombe. Although that is most surprising because Boscombe is higher than Bath Hill, it works because the tunnel is much deeper there than at the hotel – whilst the ground level rises to Boscombe, the tunnel itself slopes down from Bath Hill. Certainly, there is a much larger engineering installation at the pier than in the days of the simple outfall method, due to the terrific pumps and large sewage-holding tank. Strictly, these holding tanks are known as attenuation tanks.

If the low-level sewage collection point to the west is at the pier, the one to the east is the pumping station at Hengistbury Head, on the corner of The Broadway and Clowes Avenue, with its nearby large attenuation tank under Solent Beach car park. The old system continues to drain the locality down to a point close to sea level, and the Clowes Avenue pumps send it all back uphill to Seafield Gardens, Southbourne. From there it flows by gravity to Woodland Walk, meets up with the 'west sewage' and proceeds to Holdenhurst via Shaft One. Much of the Boscombe and Southbourne material was previously piped down to the Fisherman's Walk and Boscombe Pier outfalls – the CIS now intercepts it and directs it to Woodland Walk. The Northern Main was easily connected into Shaft One directly because it was already located in Castle Lane.

To recap, the system is mainly gravitational, including the waste intercepted from areas around Alum Chine, Middle Chine and Durley Chine. The exceptions are those uphill pipes which require pumping: from Bournemouth Pier to Bath Hill, from Boscombe Pier up Sea Road, from Iford to Seafield Gardens, and from Clowes Avenue to Seafield Gardens. As can be imagined, the whole job took some time, and the main pier's outfalls were greatly needed until 1974 when the pumps became operational. Completion was about two years later, whilst the final stage of installing the two attenuation tanks was in the 1990s after Wessex Water had taken over the operation from the council. It is notable that the ambitious and successful project was conceived and mainly built before Bournemouth lost its powerful County Borough status on 1 April 1974 due to local government reorganisation.

Although it is possible to plan for foul water quantities, the same cannot be said for surface water. But it is simply uneconomic to design a town's drainage system for extreme weather events because of the sheer size of the potential surface water flows. As there can be floods when the drains and tanks are completely full, a combined system is less satisfactory in principle than one having total separation between foul and surface water. However, Bournemouth adopted a practical solution: to keep the outfalls in place for very heavy weather, secure in the knowledge that their use would be rare. In other words, since the foul content of a combined system is stable, any overflow into Poole Bay (due to continuous heavy rain) is mainly the unobjectionable surface water. Wessex Water, which took over the system in 1994, carry out regular coastal sampling for water-borne bacteria. The company also now release real-time reports about use of the outfalls due to extreme weather.

In order to meet river quality standards, Holdenhurst is designed to fully treat ordinary foul sewage, including storm flow for lesser storms. As a buffer against more rain, the works contain massive storm tanks capable of holding 21,000 cubic metres. Still, larger storms are managed using the CIS. Since the tunnels are usually only part full, a penstock or valve in Shaft One can be used to hold back the flow. When this is done, the tunnels progressively fill up, creating another 10,000 cubic metres of storage in total. If exceptional rain causes them to fill up completely, the huge attenuation tanks at Bournemouth Pier and Hengistbury Head are used. Their function is temporarily to contain the increasingly diluted sewage.

If there is sufficient rain in a short time, however, even these tanks become full and their screened overflows then allow excess sewage to be passed to sea through the old outfalls. Such waste has been greatly diluted, and solid material greater than 6mm is retained in the sewer system by the fine screens. Moreover, it complies with the national consent conditions laid down by the Environment Agency. The technique is justifiable because the only alternatives would involve sewage backing up into properties, or a design costing billions that would come into play perhaps once in 100 years! Furthermore, these events are usually occasions of stormy weather when the diluted sewage is swiftly dissipated. Nonetheless, the surfing community must find the company's real-time reports very helpful. Once conditions have returned to normal, relatively small pumps in the attenuation tanks return their contents back to the main system so that they can revert to their usual empty state.

And finally, the *pièce de résistance*: the below-ground pumping hall at Bournemouth Pier. It is very well disguised with double-door access from beneath the western buttress to the flyover, by the approach to the pier. The buttress plaque, unveiled on 27 March 1974, refers to the town's sewage being sent inland to purification works and no longer polluting the sea. Fig. 17 shows a general view of three of the four powerful pumps alongside the walkway on the right. The fourth pump nearest to the viewpoint is out of shot. One of the four is never in use, being on standby. The other three can send 750 litres of sewage up Bath Hill every second, a sobering thought indeed. The pumps are placed on standby by rotation, in order to keep all four in good working condition.

At the time of inspection on a dry afternoon, the three pumps available for use were mainly silent. But once sufficient foul sewage had built up in the separate collection area adjoining the hall, one (or more) burst into life automatically, making it difficult to carry on a conversation. The other loud noise came from the electric fan blowing fresh air into the hall through the enormous ducting and grill that can be seen in the photograph at the back of the hall. The fan's purpose is to combat methane for safety reasons.

The collection area contains a grit channel and two wet wells which allow grit (and most of the other items which could damage the pumps) to drop out of suspension – some fifty tons or so are removed from the settlement tank every six months. Alongside the wall to the left of the picture is the pipe, served by all four pumps and used to send the sewage up Bath Hill. Should there be a need for maintenance or replacement of any plant and machinery, the travelling crane can be used to hoist it up to ground level. The safe working load of three tonnes is sufficient for all needs.

Sewage holding tank at appoach to Bournemouth Pier
The tank is located beneath the circular paved area in front of the fairground ride. The BIC is on the right and the West Cliff is straight ahead. (Author's collection)

The underground location of the attenuation tank can be easily identified within the area between the western buttress to the flyover and the pier entrance. It lies directly beneath the large circle of stone-type paviors which have a lighter colour than the surrounding hard surfacing. Due to this pedestrian area being so busy during the day, a 7.30 a.m. inspection was needed in order to measure the tank's diameter; it is 20.8m or 68ft 3in. The stone-type paviors have been laid with some artistry, and there is a sweeping swirl of brick paviors and an adjacent stripe running from one edge of the circle to the other. The whole appearance is as far removed from the concept of a sewage-holding area as can be imagined, and in such a location, rightly so.

The tank has a usable capacity of 1,200 cubic metres. This is 80 per cent of its total size and the stage at which the old outfalls are automatically triggered. The pumps are not able to pump more than 750 litres per second into the CIS at the top of Bath Hill; flows in excess of this arriving at the pumping station are therefore diverted to the tank. If extreme conditions cause all the CIS tunnels to fill up completely, the pumps here may be unable to remove the sewage at their normal maximum of 750 litres per second, so again excess flows would be diverted to the tank. To give an idea of the facility, the attenuation tank would be a 'holding buffer' for around thirty minutes at 750 litres per second, before the old outflows are used.

Summing up, this is an extraordinary system of town drainage that strikes the essential balance between cost and need. It was obviously desirable to stop the outflow of raw sewage into the seawater at what is arguably the best beach in the country. Equally, to make the CIS with larger tunnels or have even more enormous attenuation tanks would have been at prohibitive cost. In any case, the force of nature means that there would be no guarantee of never having to use the old outfalls. The old County Borough made an excellent job of reversing the direction of Bournemouth's sewage and treating it so well that the residue flows past Christchurch unnoticed.

TWENTY-TWO

Undercliff Drive Monster

After Bournemouth was made a County Borough in 1900, an Undercliff Drive was seriously considered – both to protect against undue sea erosion and to provide a promenade. Many thought that such a sea wall and promenade would solve everything: cliff erosion would stop, people would be able to walk along the beautiful coastline in comfort, and the council's agreement with the Lord of the Manor would be fulfilled. Under that agreement, Bournemouth Council was committed to take action within ten years to 'keep up the cliffs' or lose their ground lease on the shore and cliffs. If the council did not take action in time, the owner could break the lease and regain the property. It would probably then be sold on to a developer to make a profit rather than be used to care for the town. However, due to the high expected cost of keeping up the cliffs, there was naturally some opposition from ratepayers, who were expected to finance such an expensive scheme. The Residents' Association were thus highly against it.

A local newspaper, the *Bournemouth Graphic*, was very good at publishing cartoons that told a story. Although this one is a classic example of a political issue in a picture, there is one strange feature – it relates to Greek mythology. Let us take a highly simplified look at the myth of Perseus and Andromeda. Perseus, the son of Zeus, had borrowed some winged sandals and was flying over Ethiopia when he saw Andromeda chained to a rock or cliff at the ocean's edge. Having fallen in love at once with the pretty maiden, he enquired of her plight by speaking to a nearby couple who turned out to be her parents, the King and Queen of Ethiopia. They explained that Andromeda was to be a human sacrifice for the giant sea serpent, Cetus – a creature who destroyed both man and beast. It seems that when the Queen had unwisely proclaimed herself to be more beautiful than the sea goddesses (Nereids), they had become annoyed and complained to the sea god Poseidon. He had accepted the complaint as well-founded, threatening to flood the country in reprisal. Still worse, he ordered an attack by Cetus, who could only be placated by the sacrifice of Andromeda.

Andromeda's parents were distraught by their plan to sacrifice their daughter in order to save their country. The mother must have been especially tortured by the cause of the impending tragedy – her own vanity. When Perseus proposed that

Undercliff Drive Scheme – a monster from Greek mythology
The arguments are made for and against a proposal to keep up the cliffs and help tourism.
(*Bournemouth Graphic* cartoon, courtesy of the Beales Archive)

he slay the monster and marry their daughter, a greatly relieved King and Queen immediately agreed. Perseus flew over to the hungry Cetus as he was swimming to the shore and decapitated him in the water. He then freed Andromeda and married her. However, there ensued a quarrel with her previous fiancé, who was also her uncle. Perseus solved this issue neatly during a battle (in a dining room, of all places) by turning his rival into stone. To achieve this feat, he only needed to show Medusa's head to Andromeda's uncle. His reasons for having decapitated Medusa, and many other aspects of the story, are not relevant enough to include here.

Before relating the Greek myth to the *Graphic*'s Bournemouth version of it, some press coverage from 1904 is of interest. Early comment referred to the Residents' Association's attitude in uncomplimentary terms such as 'piteously imbecile' and 'crass ignorance'. The Association's contention had conveniently ignored the contractual commitment of the town to keep up the cliffs. In addition, the Riviera and other watering places with promenades showed a public demand for an Undercliff Drive. If the Lord of the Manor did regain the land, it could be a goldmine for the few but would be to the detriment of the town. A later edition lamented the overuse of printer's ink in the matter and the 'speculative random jabber made by prejudiced individuals'. Not only that, but people were 'running amok' over it and making themselves look ridiculous. Editorial, in favour of the scheme, continued relentlessly.

On a more positive note, a fresh start on the whole issue was then made by a Ratepayers' League meeting that resembled more 'Advance Bournemouth' than 'Down with everything'. The idea was to gather together all ratepayers in favour of two things: firstly, protecting the cliffs with an Undercliff Drive and promenade, and secondly, investing in a pavilion, reading rooms, cafés, concert room and general all-weather facilities second to none in the country. The League definitely wanted the cliffs to be kept up, to prevent the alternative of a big speculative building scheme that would be a disaster for the town.

The value of the cartoon was ostensibly more to concentrate minds in order to aid the debate than give a ready-made opinion. Yet it is a little hard to come down on the side of the swordsman. Clearly, Andromeda is chained to the attractive cliffs of Bournemouth whilst Perseus has arrived from the sky with his sword, marked Residents' Association. Indeed, she personifies the cliffs whilst Perseus personifies the Residents' Association. She says: 'Oh! Save me from this monster.' He replies: 'Fear not, beauteous maiden. Altho' perchance my sword may not be strong enough to break the brute's back, I'll protect thee at all cost.' Not only is there a grim sea monster marked UNDER CLIFF DRIVE on the sands, there is another monster at the cliff top marked OVER CLIFF DRIVE. He is speaking to his low-level friend, saying: 'Go ahead Chummy. Spoil her beauty for her. I've rooted up trees & knocked the place about up here & swallowed Twenty thousand pounds. You've gorged £45,000. So between us and the Corporation we ought to jolly well wreck Bournemouth.'

Questions for debate spring to mind. Is the town going to spend beyond the means of its captive ratepayers and thereby wreck itself? Would the beauty of the cliffs be lost if an Undercliff Drive were to be built? Did the residents (like Perseus) only truly appreciate the beauty of the natural cliffs (personified by Andromeda) for the first time when they were faced with expense? At the very least, should a start not be made on such a wise long-term investment purely for the tourist base of the town? There must have been vigorous debate in the town but the sea wall and promenade was indeed built over the years in sections from the Poole boundary to Solent Road, Southbourne; its contribution to the success of the resort has been immense. The first section opened on 6 November 1907, an occasion regarded as a personal triumph by major proponent Sir Merton Russell-Cotes. At the same time, he and his wife gave the town East Cliff Hall and their collection, now the Russell-Cotes Art Gallery & Museum.

Bournemouth now has a better case for seeking grants to maintain its sea defences than any other town on the south coast. If coast protection measures fail, the sea wall and promenades would go first, followed by cliff erosion and the loss of roads and buildings at the cliff top. As argued in effect by the *Bournemouth Graphic*, the Undercliff Drive was indeed essential both for 'keeping up the cliffs' and for tourism. It never was a monster.

TWENTY-THREE

Smuggling at Fisherman's Walk

A letter was written to the *Echo* in May 1948 by Mr T. Gurney Stedman about a smuggler's exploit, so confirming the local legend – Fisherman's Walk was indeed a route for contraband. Prompted by the planned auction sale of woodland at the junction of Southbourne Road and Southbourne Grove, the writer found himself thinking of those faraway days when there was a smugglers' track on the west side of the land being sold. Although there is still a small area of amenity woodland at that road corner, the western side of the site has long since been redeveloped as a block of flats amongst trees. Unsurprisingly, no visible track survives.

Mr Stedman then went on to relate his early childhood memories of delighting in the stories of two old men, Bill Marshall and George Dorey. There is some confirmation of these two men in the census returns for Pokesdown. William Marshall, a farm worker, was recorded as married with six children in 1841, but the three eldest had left home as adults by 1851. George Dorey was away from home in 1841 but is shown as married with four children in 1851. These dates are consistent with the following story, occurring around 1820.

Bill Marshall was a 'tough guy', as evidenced by an 'ear split to pieces by a policeman's truncheon, but that's another story'. There was a kind of little goat path that had been cut out of the cliff at the end of Fisherman's Walk and led to the beach. Late at night, a smuggler would signal from the path to an incoming ship that the coast was clear. The method was to have a lantern fastened to a leather belt and concealed beneath a reefer jacket, which was a double-breasted woollen coat worn by sailors. By lifting a corner of the jacket, the light would be seen and a boat would come in to land the goods. Soon, the locals would be climbing the goat path with the contraband on their shoulders and then rush to meet a pair-horse van waiting for them on Christchurch Road.

On this particular night, Marshall was nearly caught with a heavy load of tobacco. Before he got as far as the van, a 'pal' was waiting to warn him that 'Preventive' men were about. Clearly, the landing had taken place when the coast was not clear after all. Instead of taking his usual route, Marshall diverted to what is 'now' Sunnyhill Road and to some huge elm trees opposite what is 'now' the Reliance Laundry in Paisley Road. He then hid the goods in the tree roots. It seems that these roads were identified to give the reader some idea of location only, and 'now' refers to the letter date in 1948. Arrangements were made for the van to return a few days later. After the tobacco was put aboard, Marshall's successful night's work was complete and he received the normal payment of 7s 6d.

TWENTY-FOUR

Growing Pains

*I*n spite of Bournemouth's success, the town nevertheless suffered some problems along the way. Maybe the frontier nature of fast growth in such a beautiful location made the growing pains a little strange.

The early town boasted a really quaint footbridge supported by pine poles and covered in greenery. Early maps mark it as the Rustic Bridge, a much-loved and much-photographed structure running from Gervis Place through to Old Christchurch Road, which was then North Road. As a sort of passing place for pedestrians, an alcove existed halfway across the bridge. One could stop here at a point immediately above where a stream had run at the bottom of a ravine known as Church Glen. The bridge was considered necessary in order to connect Ashley Villas, North Road, with the prestigious Westover Road and its sixteen large villas, completed by 1840. Everything being so new, perhaps it was about the only truly quaint feature to be seen in town. Church Glen has long since been totally covered over by development and completely disappeared from view. For instance, the department store, Beales, has been built above it.

It was Thomas Shettle, one of the early Bournemouth Commissioners, who owned Ashley Villas and built the bridge for his tenants to use in 1853. However, it was also convenient for others who were charged a halfpenny toll for the privilege of avoiding the detour to the bottom of the hill and back up Gervis Place. Alternatively, they would have to go via Hinton Road, which itself bridged the Glen. Hence the town centre of the early 1860s saw an attractive 20ft ravine spanned by a most eye-catching footbridge, adorned by climbing plants and giving views of Church Glen, St Peter's Church and of the other side of the Bourne Stream, including Portman Lodge. No wonder the development next described was criticised at the time for spoiling 'one of the most picturesque spots in Bournemouth'.

When, in 1866, builder Henry Joy replaced the Rustic Bridge with the Arcade, it was soon christened 'Joy's Folly'. Many thought it sheer madness to remove the Rustic Bridge and build some shops across a ravine. 'Was there not a level site he could have used?' people would have said, and, 'We don't want to lose our lovely footbridge!' At the start, the new premises with their large basements were slow to be occupied. However, when the popularity of the scheme was finally ensured in 1873 by the provision of a most fetching glass roof, Joy's vision and acumen had

Rustic Bridge provides site for Bournemouth Arcade
Before Henry Joy built the Arcade over Church Glen in 1866, this picturesque footbridge ran from Gervis Place to Old Christchurch Road. (Courtesy of Bournemouth Libraries)

to be recognised. The Arcade remains a success to this day, conveniently linking Westover Road (once known as the Bond Street of Bournemouth) with the prime part of Old Christchurch Road shops. No doubt some strong objectors from 1866 were happy to use the new shops.

In another case, the nation is depicted as telling the town that it needs to do more. A humorous cartoon, headed 'Hard Times', is here reproduced from an issue of the *Bournemouth Graphic*.

> JOHN BULL: 'Well. How are you getting on down here? Caught many this season?'
> MR BOURNEMOUTH: 'No! Times are very bad – not what they were even when I only had the seagull and sand martin to attract 'em. Now I'm giving them up-to-date decoy birds, I only seem to catch a few miserable sparrows. Can't seem to attract any 'hoof' birds nowadays.'
> J.B.: 'Perhaps you put too much salt on their tails when you did catch them. Strikes me, now you've gone in for classy decoys, you'd better go further, and get a Pier Pavilion bird or a Kursaal!!'

One of the birds, marked GODFREY, is clearly the famous conductor of the Municipal Orchestra, Sir Dan Godfrey, whilst another bird, marked GOLF, has a set of clubs. Generally, the holidaymaker birds have suitcases and are as free as the air – they could easily, perish the thought, go to a competing resort! Apart from music and golf, the main ways of 'trapping' the holidaymakers included the pier and steamboats, the Undercliff and Overcliff Drives and charabancs. Yet the incentives were not enough, as indicated by the most unhappy boarding-house proprietor representing the business interests of the town.

Hard Times – John Bull converses with a hard-pressed businessman
A succinct debate is held about how to recover and promote profitable trade in the town. (*Bournemouth Graphic* cartoon, courtesy of the Beales Archive)

Having suffered as a ratepayer due to the expensive improvements and seen a drop in trade for his pains, Mr Bournemouth is looking even less happy perhaps when he gets John Bull's advice to spend more on even better decoys. If there was a pavilion on the pier or a brand new kursaal (amusement park) would that gain him more lodgers? The reference to 'salt on their tails' must be to the false folklore that it would prevent a bird from taking off again, or even make it become your pet. Maybe the town was *too* anxious to increase trade by ladling on too much salt and creating some sales resistance amongst its visitors – but if so, why is John Bull advising more of the same? He could be saying that Bournemouth has yet to achieve critical mass, and further tourist spending would prove very successful. Again we see the issue of faith in the future. There could be different interpretations. No doubt it rang a bell, particularly with those who felt they were suddenly being exposed to excessive costs through the rates. In a nutshell, we can see that times were hard for the resort and a solution was imperative for economic survival. Luckily, Bournemouth has always specialised in economic survival.

In a way, the examples of local problems mentioned above are not a cause for gloom – rather, they show that hard work, optimism, and faith in the future have always been endemic in the town. Yet the final instance to be recounted is to do with the darker side of human nature, and the significant resentment of some in the Victorian working class.

On Bonfire Night in 1884, crowds gathered in the town centre looking for trouble and greatly outnumbering the police. They included those who had been 'pulled up', to use their words, for different offences through the year and may have been looking for revenge. Police knew trouble was likely and drafted in a number of constables from outlying areas. During the day it was fairly quiet, but by 8 p.m., when the rains had cleared, there was a concerted move from all parts of town to the favourite trouble spot of the Triangle. Reportedly, the increasingly excited and dense horde was drawn from out-of-town areas and included many navvies working on the new railway line. A tar barrel was soon rolled down the hill towards the town centre, followed by a shouting rabble.

When the barrel was being taken back up the hill, presumably in order for the crowd to have more of the same entertainment, Police Sergeant Brewer attempted to seize it but failed. Not only was it kicked away from him, but also, he needed the help of two constables to prevent him being mobbed on the spot. Around 11 p.m., when we can safely assume that a lot of alcohol had been drunk, two or three barrels were sent down Commercial Road, resulting in a collision between two or three constables and the ringleaders. When one man was struck on the head, sticks were freely used against the police, who were forced to retreat at full speed along Terrace Road.

At this stage, any residual sense of restraint disappeared. Within minutes, the uproarious mob surged down the hill, throwing stones and bricks through nearly every non-shuttered window. The damage was estimated at several hundred pounds. Mr Johnson, the grocer of Commercial Road, suffered some threats and was rumoured to have left town during the disturbance – in 1882, he had prosecuted one of the rioters. A constable, disguised as a labourer, was recognised and severely mauled in a back street. A press report commended the police for not interfering any more than necessary because, had they done so, somebody would have been injured – the mob only wanted the police to start first.

Bournemouth did have some growing pains related to its fast and sometimes difficult expansion as a resort. However, they were very minor indeed when set against the merit of the bright new town which materialised; that early faith in the future was proven to be fully justified.

TWENTY-FIVE

World Record for One Day

B ournemouth holds the distinction of hosting a flying event that produced a new world record at Meyrick Park – for one day only on 11 April 1914. A popular but rather diffident man, Gustav Hamel was a pioneer along with the best of them. Fascinated as he was by the challenges of early powered flight, he knew the risks and tragically died in its pursuit. Being tall, modest, quiet in nature with blue eyes and wavy hair, he was the darling of the crowds.

Hamel was mainly noted for being the first pilot to deliver official airmail in September 1911 as part of the Coronation celebrations for King George V: from Hendon to the Postmaster General at Windsor, a flight of 21 miles covered in just 12.5 minutes. It averaged 101mph, compared to the winner of the speed competition

Gustav Hamel (1889-1914) with lady passenger in Meyrick Park, April 1914
The popular pilot thrilled the crowds at this display with his aerobatics.

Hamel carrying out the manoeuvre which became a world record
For one day, 11 April 1914, he held the record of twenty-one consecutive loop the loops.

at the Bournemouth International Aviation Meeting the previous year, who covered the five circuits of 8.92 miles total in 13.53 minutes, i.e. 40mph only. Although circuits must be slower than a direct flight, it still shows an enormous technical advance over the year.

In April 1913, Hamel made another influential flight, one which clearly demonstrated the value of aircraft in time of war for reconnaissance and bombing. His non-stop journey with a passenger was reported by the *New York Herald*: from Dover to Cologne, 245 miles in 258 minutes, and encountering five rainstorms along the way. Next January, he took up Miss Trehawke Davies and looped the loop, making her the first woman in the world to experience the manoeuvre. In February 1914, Hamel was at Windsor Castle looping the loop for King George V. Having done fourteen continuous loops with ease and grace, he had a lengthy conversation with a fascinated king.

The one-day world record was achieved at Meyrick Park, Bournemouth, where he was billed to perform sensational displays of upside-down flying and looping the loop on two separate days, 8 and 11 April 1914. The events were to be from 3.30 p.m. to 5 p.m., the admissions 1s to 5s, and there was to be a draw for a passenger flight. The enthusiastic crowd, estimated at 5,000 to 6,000, thronged the area around the flying green and was delighted by the displays. But a world-record attempt was not expected. On the second day, Hamel took a passenger for a thrilling ride just a few feet above the sands and sea, and 'jumped' Bournemouth Pier before returning to the park at 110mph. Another passenger was the twenty-two-year-old Prince Maurice of Battenberg, who was to die for Britain later in the year at Ypres. Referring to the loop, he said, 'I felt no sensation as we turned over. It was a good loop.' A certain Mrs Knocker of Alderholt was favoured by flights on both days.

A few minutes after 4 p.m., Hamel began the record attempt after he made particularly certain of being well strapped into the cockpit. Superlatives were scattered through the newspaper report – superb exhibition; resembled a swallow; audience held their breath; the aviator and his machine resembled a huge bird tumbling over and over; crammed with thrills for the onlookers. After fifteen minutes of display, starting from 2,500ft altitude, Hamel glided beautifully to earth to a rapturous reception. A new world record had been set: twenty-one loops.

Perfectly in character, the unassuming pilot proceeded to speak quite casually about his great achievement. He said that he had had a most enjoyable afternoon and felt he had given some good sport to the people of Bournemouth. Apparently, it was difficult to rise from the ground and it would have been better if the land had been 100ft higher. (Enquiries in the aviation field have failed to find an explanation for this remark.) He also objected to some spectators avoiding the entry charge by parking outside the gate of the park. All in all, it seems that it was a somewhat routine day for him, rather than a world record-breaking day! Perhaps it was routine by his standards – the very next day he broke his own record by looping the loop twenty-two times at Hendon.

On 23 May 1914, Hamel collected a new plane from France and, despite being unhappy with the engine, set off to fly the channel; he never arrived in England. A flotilla of destroyers searched without success for two days and nights. In July, the body was found by a French fisherman and identified without doubt. The tragedy so disturbed Winston Churchill, who had been friends with Hamel, that he gave up his flying lessons until 1917. Certainly, there are some reports referring to Churchill being a passenger of Hamel during loops. In 1956, air historian Harry Harper paid tribute: 'It was he who set an example that all those others followed so finely and so well. He was ready to risk everything, even life itself, to get that letter through to the King.'

However much it may now seem a cliché, flying before the First World War really was a case of 'Those Magnificent Men in Their Flying Machines'.

TWENTY-SIX

Strange Case of the Beales Fire

here is a curious randomness about how people's lives are impacted in serious ways though the agency of Lady Luck, and here is a case in point. The account which follows is a piecing-together of sources and recollections but is believed to be generally accurate. Before fire broke out on Monday, 7 November 1966 at Beales department store, both the Chief Constable and the Chief Fire Officer were present at a Rotary lunch at the Pavilion. A fire appliance was returning to the Central fire station in Holdenhurst Road, and Beales was serving its customers in the usual way. A quantity of fireworks had been left over from Bonfire Night but everything seemed normal.

The first strange thing to occur was when a temporary member of staff said, 'I wonder what would happen if I put a match in this box of fireworks.' At the time, the fireworks were being packed away to store in zinc-lined tea chests in order to go on sale again in twelve months. It is believed that a rocket caught light and very soon there was a succession of bangs in that part of the department store. A number of rockets whizzed around to the accompaniment of screaming from mothers. One eyewitness mentioned that, from a distance, the banging sounded as if there were problems with the mechanics of a lift. Very soon, the sprinkler system activated and the fire brigade was called. Both the Chief Fire Officer and the Chief Constable, who were 'in mufti', arrived from the Pavilion. Nigel and Anthony Beale attended, but Norman and Frank Beale were out of town that day.

Firemen with ladders had to smash the windows on upper levels of the building to get at those trapped, including children. Some thirty frightened shoppers were rescued from the windows and taken down the ladders to the road below. A woman with a baby said, 'I don't want to go through that again. Nobody could see anything. All I could hear were screams and explosions.' Another remarked, 'It was just like a battlefield.' Three children were rescued before the arrival of the firemen, when a woman thrust her hand through the smoke at a window and passed them down to a man standing on a van roof, who had stopped to help whilst on his way to a job interview. Amazingly, the fire caused no serious injury, although fifteen were taken to hospital.

The sprinklers saved the store. Ironically, having done so, the fire damage proved much less expensive to rectify than the water damage. The fire may not have taken

Fireworks at Beales in 1966
For no known reason, a member of staff started the fire by lighting a match in a box of fireworks.
Thankfully, there were no deaths or serious injuries. (Courtesy of the *Bournemouth Echo*)

Beales from the parapet of St Peter's Church
The department store was rebuilt after a direct hit in the Second World War. (Author's collection)

hold, but the water reacted with the sulphur in the fireworks to create a very dense black smoke, so dense that it was not possible to see your hand in front of your face. This is the reason that people were escaping though the windows. They simply could not find their way through the building to an exit.

At the very end of the fire and rescue work, the woman who had caused it was found wandering in a daze on the roof of the store. Understandably, the trauma meant that she was not fit to work for some weeks. Mr Beale did a roll-call of staff in St Peter's graveyard nearby and pointed out how fortunate everyone was. Indeed, the number of fireworks in stock was only a fraction of those held a few days earlier. Had the fire happened then, it would have been much more serious.

A decision was taken by Beales never to sell fireworks from that day forward – and nor have they.

TWENTY-SEVEN

Ensbury Manor, Smuggling and Ghosts

*U*ntil demolition in 1936, there is not much doubt that Ensbury Manor, also known as Ensbury House, was the oldest house in Bournemouth. For a long time, this large and rambling property had been vacant and falling into disrepair. It was located just west of the junction of Wimborne Road with New Road leading to Ferndown. The residential redevelopment of the 8-acre site, creating Avebury Avenue, Cedar Avenue and Austen Avenue, has since been described as one of the greatest acts of sacrilege in the history of Bournemouth. At the time, however, there seemed little protest. In March 1936, the *Echo* reported on the proposed scheme with a photograph of the old ivy-covered homestead, and remarked that part was believed to be about 700 years old.

Originally, the house was part of a large estate. There were two late eighteenth-century wings of stucco-covered brick walls with tiled roofs, and Venetian windows on the ground floor. There was also a Victorian addition and some older parts at the rear. Internally, the house was a maze of passages and funny-shaped rooms. An 1868 advertisement described the accommodation as including front hall, four sitting rooms, five best and six servants' bedrooms, commodious offices, stables and other premises, gardens, lawns, croquet grounds, shooting and fishing. A major feature was the intricately carved oak Jacobean fireplace, which reached 15ft from floor to ceiling (18ft in one report) and was felt to be one of the finest in the country. Perhaps unsurprisingly, it 'disappeared' when the house came down. Another description, from 1936, mentioned that 'Two staircases with delightful turns and twists add to the puzzle of its riot of nooks and corners. An explorer in its upper apartments is held in a constant state of expectancy'.

When the site was cleared, two underground chambers were found and also some tunnelling, thereby (as it always does) raising the question of smuggling. One of the chambers was 6.5ft long by 5ft deep, well built in brick and capable of holding a considerable number of small brandy tubs, or even of hiding two or three men. According to legend, the house was used by a daring band of Free Traders, and tunnels existed to connect, in some way, to smuggling activities known to have occurred at Kinson churchyard. As with many such theories, it is circumstantial evidence and pure speculation only – none of the builders actually investigated the matter by trying to go through a tunnel at the time of demolition. A lady living

Ensbury Manor
The 1936 demolition of this old house has been described as sacrilege. (Courtesy of Bournemouth Libraries)

nearby pointed out that the chambers could have been ice boxes and the tunnelling to do with old drainage facilities.

An even less convincing tale concerns the 1930s owner of Ensbury Manor. He was trying to sink some posts in the garden but came upon a solid barrier – a large mental leap is needed to see this as evidence of a cellar for contraband. In Cedar Avenue, there remains an enormous Cedar of Lebanon tree (protected by a Tree Preservation Order), which stood alongside Ensbury Manor and can easily be seen today from Wimborne Road. It towers so far above the adjoining houses that it is completely out of scale, yet at the same time adds character to the street scene.

The Austen family occupied the house from 1840 to 1890, after which there was a succession of tenants. The governess for one of them wrote wistfully of 1900, when there was wildfowling, punting on the river Stour, and wagonette journeys to Moyles Court in the New Forest. At a servants' Christmas party a gramophone was hired from Bournemouth, 3 miles away. It had 'an enormous horn and funny wind cylinders'. Another tenant turned the dining room into a chapel for local Catholics, who were summoned to prayer by a bell at the back of the house. Thousands of sightseers responded to the newspaper report of the demolition of this haunted manor house on the northern edge of town. Sometimes the crowds were so great that the police had to be present.

Cedar of Lebanon tree, Ensbury Manor
This magnificent specimen is all that survives from the grounds of the thirteenth-century manor house.
(Author's collection)

But what can we say of the hauntings? If you go along the three avenues today, you
see merely an ordinary pre-war scheme of medium-density residential development,
with the only surprising note being the massive tree. Indeed, when the manor was due
to come down, the *Echo* predicted that nothing would be left as a reminder of its past,
steeped as it was in mystery and romance. As for atmosphere, by 1936 the old place
may have seemed abandoned, weird and something of a ghost's playground. It was
said that the pungent essence of ancient days enveloped it – or at least so it may have
seemed to anyone susceptible to suggestion.

Folklore claimed that an unseen presence transfixed its subjects with a rustle of
silk and a draught of cold air. A former resident is reputed to have seen a ghost from
the deep: 'A tall figure with a grim, sallow face, waiting, alert in dripping oilskins,
but leaving no mark on the floor.' Tales have been told of terrified maids, whose
bedclothes were 'snatched from them by the unseen hand of a malevolent spectre'
while they slept in the attic. When the roof was being removed by the builders, the
spectre of a great squawking white owl was reported as flying from an upper window
to a rookery; it screeched in protest every time another section was demolished.
However, there is a more down-to-earth explanation that has also been reported
whereby the owl (a real one) had made its home in the deserted upper rooms of the
house, was unhappy to be evicted, and actually settled in a large tree nearby. From

there, rather than being an eerie genie, it lamented the loss of its home, nothing more. Sometimes, it softly flew past the builders.

There was also a village story about a room at the manor which was always kept sealed because of some mysterious secret. Another tale was told by a Kinson man who remembered that, as a boy, he spent an evening at the house when he and a butler were the only ones there. Suddenly, a door banged and there was a distinct rustle of clothes as if someone had passed the room they occupied; the butler told him that was always happening. Perhaps the demolition was indeed sacrilege, causing the loss of a unique link between Bournemouth and antiquity … together with the attendant ghosts.

TWENTY-EIGHT

Eleven Quirks in Brief

here are many more curiosities than can be contained in a book of this size; the following examples are necessarily abbreviated.

Hidden Clock at St Peter's Church

Since the church was built in phases from 1844, the clock on the first section was rather overtaken by events. It was readily visible at the beginning, placed as it was, high on the gabled west wall. It became partly obscured when the tower was erected in 1869 (in front of the nave of the original church but separate from it). When the space between tower and nave was filled in by the western transepts in 1874, the clock was no longer visible. Indeed, the gable stonework to which it was fitted was removed and replaced by a beam between the eaves. Fig. 18 shows the 1848 clock (Thwaites & Reed, Clerkenwell) as now relocated at the north-west corner of the bell-ringers' chamber of the tower. The clock face in the picture is only the internal one used for adjustment purposes. The large main external clock face would have been parallel to it and is missing.

Pay Level of the Town's Designer and Inspector

The services of the highly respected Christopher Crabbe Creeke (Fig. 2) were invaluable to the embryo Bournemouth. Apart from supervising drainage matters in his capacity of Inspector of Nuisances, many roads were improved and laid out in a spacious fashion that still benefits the town today. He designed many buildings and made his house available for meetings of the Improvement Commissioners. Not only were plans and specifications provided but supervision was included. Nobody could say that his pay for all this, at £50 per annum from 1856 to 1868, was too high. Yet he even suggested that if his duties became lighter or less important, he would take a lower salary.

Littledown House Staircase

The famous Dean family of Bournemouth were originally yeoman farmers who became involved in banking and eventually secured a huge amount of land through

Littledown House staircase
The cantilevered staircase without visible means of support. (Courtesy of J.P. Morgan)

the Inclosure Award of 1805. When town expansion took place, the family often made sites available on very generous terms to help development, and its legacy lives on through the charity created for the town.

One unusual feature of the Georgian Littledown House, built by William Dean in the late eighteenth century, was the grand staircase – there were no visible means of support. It is believed that there is a cantilevered system which makes it safe. The staircase remains in place and J.P. Morgan kindly agreed to the photograph being taken. The refurbished and listed Littledown House is now a most attractive part of the bank's site.

Council Chamber Battles of 1904

On 3 May, the *Bournemouth Graphic*'s diarist, Pepys, reported something of a fracas:

… Much high words and foul despiteful speaking upon the matter of a tree that was shifted during the laying of asphalte in the Holdenhurst Road, and was planted at length in Alderman Davis' garden. The Mayor did hotly rule that as the charge was laid, it was a mean imputation and base, whereat several members taking it amiss, there followed the greatest disorder that I ever saw. And in fine they parted for lunch, but being thence returned the quarrel was renewed, so that I was almost out of my wits with trouble, and especially Mr Gunning, being all in confusion and filled with bad humours, did so far forget himself as to rip out everything most unworthily on the Mayor, calling him in a word a cad, and in all manner most ill-conditioned and discourteous. So at the last the Mayor did threaten to resign, and would have done so incontinently had not the council assured him of their high esteem … And

Mr Gunning did apologise very freely ... Was nevertheless a most humiliating thing to say ... A quarrel in the Sanitary Committee meeting ... Not till he had taken back his wish that members of the type of Mr Wilson should give place to better men that the business of the council could proceed ... Do suffer themselves to utter words in the heat of passion and excitement as heedlessly as though they were foxed with wine.

Piano Stranded on Boscombe Pier

One well-known defence measure of the Second World War was the destruction in July 1940 of the centres of both piers in order to prevent their possible use by Hitler. At this time of great urgency, due to the risk of invasion, the army duly set the explosives and blew up a 120ft-section of Boscombe Pier. Mrs Joan Harrington has kindly supplied an eyewitness account. She recalls hearing a very loud bang. Unfortunately, no one had ensured that the municipal upright piano was moved to the land. To the amusement of many, some time later a boat was used by the army to rescue the piano, deliver it to the shore and back into the hands of the council.

Boscombe Pier was blown up by the army in 1940
After this anti-invasion measure was taken, the army had to conduct a sea rescue of the council's piano. (Courtesy of Bournemouth Libraries)

1840s Bournemouth – Idyll or Nightmare?

The 1840 town guide paints a picture of perfection with many a glowing phrase: the gay resort of fashion and the favoured retreat of the invalid; genial temperature at all seasons; tranquil retirement that may here be successfully sought; invigorating repose; best protection against ennui; spots where before no sound was heard but the rustling of the rank grass and the wild shrub as they waved in the light sea breeze, etc. Much subsequent comment has followed in the same vein to promote the town.

Yet even the wealthy new residents could encounter the harsh distress of the poverty of the times and be affected by it. Perhaps the best local example is the rich Talbot family, who had a property on the East Cliff and experienced small crowds of the poor gathering under their windows throwing sticks and stones. 'Give us work, we are starving,' they shouted. It was the inspiration for Georgina Talbot to try to do something about it when she later inherited some money. She bought land and founded Talbot Village in the middle of the nineteenth century, on a Victorian-style self-help basis, with tenants having a house and 1 acre. In short, despite the flowery language of the guide, 1840s Bournemouth was certainly not Utopia for all.

Why Only One 'Street' in the Town

Part of the early town's image was to have no streets at all, and it remains a current boast. However, not everyone is aware of the exception, which occurs courtesy of the 'founding' Tregonwells. Orchard Street runs by the current Primark to Commercial Road from Terrace Road. It originally adjoined an orchard marked on the 1835 map a little to the west of the bridge over The Brook (*see* Chapter Eighteen), and survived until at least 1851. Tended by the family's gardener living nearby in Terrace Cottage, it is almost certainly named after that orchard. But there is no real explanation of why it alone evaded the town's 'no street' rule, or why it continues to do so.

Hengistbury Head's Ghostly Horseman

There is a surprising sequel to the spectre described in *Hengistbury Head: The Whole Story* (*see* Bibliography). A manager at the *Echo* had suffered some ribbing about his reported 'spectral sighting' at 6 a.m. one morning in 1982 on the south side of Christchurch Harbour. The manager's parents had also seen the apparition about a month earlier. The ghostly rider had collar-length hair, was unkempt and wore a flared jacket in the seventeenth-century style with protruding sleeves. He vanished in seconds.

When researching another matter, I had a meeting with Mike Parker from the old-established family of fishermen in Christchurch. He told me that he had read the earlier book *after* having had a similar experience in the same location himself. Unfortunately, however, he had always kept it a secret – it would not have been taken seriously and he would never have been allowed to forget it!

Life Copies Fiction at the Shelley Theatre

Percy Shelley was an enthusiastic producer of plays in the small theatre, which remains part of the recent redevelopment at Boscombe Manor. From the camera's viewpoint at the back of the large stage, the need for refurbishment is clear. Although that will not be completed until 2014, the developers have already had a very successful trial performance in the existing shell of a theatre. In October 2010, the Dorset Corset Theatre Co. put on *Frankenstein: The Year Without a Summer*. Four nights of packed houses for the 170-seat playhouse are encouraging for the future.

On 26 December 1852, a play called *The Wreck Ashore* was being performed for the usual appreciative local audience. But unbeknown to the players, a real-life drama was unfolding on Boscombe Beach. There was a real wreck ashore after a ship had broken clear of her moorings at Studland and been blown east to Boscombe; the *William Glen Anderson* had foundered. During the play's performance, an unconscious Norwegian sailor was carried into the building for treatment; he was kindly dealt with and left sleeping. When morning came he had disappeared, never to be seen again. Sea conditions were rough and the ship was a complete wreck. Sadly, although no seamen from the wrecked ship drowned, the lifeboat from Shelley's yacht attempted to help, capsized, and one of its crew could not be rescued.

Shelley Theatre, Boscombe. To be refurbished and reopened
Sir Percy Florence Shelley (1819-1889) produced many popular plays here in the nineteenth century. (Courtesy of Charles Higgins Partnership)

Folly or Ornament?

Was the water tower (Fig. 19) in the Upper Gardens built without any real purpose in a way typical of an eighteenth-century folly? Would it be fair, instead, to judge it as a most attractive ornament to complement the beauty of its surroundings? Having seen it, the temptation might be to answer both questions with a 'Yes'. There it stands as a visual incident within the total scene, yet without any use that is evident or appears probable.

The eminent architect Decimus Burton was responsible for the tower in the late nineteenth century. As a very practical man, he did indeed have a clear purpose in mind. In the early days of the town, the Bourne Stream was notorious for being very swampy and in places even 'lake-like'. To combat that undesirable state, broken pottery was taken from the clay works higher up the valley and laid down on both sides of the stream to provide adequate drainage. The force of the current in the stream was enough to drive a water wheel and fill a high-level tank in the water tower, so giving a head of water to irrigate flowerbeds and supply a fountain. Fig. 20 is the original ornamental feature in action within a circular pond. Despite the freezing conditions and abundance of ice, the fountain was still working in this photograph.

Before its ground-level entrance was bricked up for security reasons, the tower was only used for storing garden tools. All the machinery has been taken out leaving the inside as a bare shell, occupied only by a colony of bats. We might say that the water tower was never a folly due to its practical initial use, but it has always been an ornament due to its pleasing design – no doubt the bats are indifferent to both issues.

Man in Green and Black

Joseph Cutler was a builder and most energetic Commissioner of the early town. Sometimes he was controversial but, like many enterprising people, he worked hard to achieve results. Born in a public house as the son of a Christchurch fisherman, apprenticed as a plumber and later joining the Australian gold rush, he returned to the country to work in London. He came to Bournemouth in 1865 on medical advice due to a breakdown in health, but worked as foreman for another builder and then very soon on his own account. He built the Durley Dene in 1866, fired a twenty-one-gun salute for the Queen's birthday in 1875, donated sixty chestnut trees for the Invalids' Walk in 1881, was helped out by subscription when his bathing machines were lost in an 1883 storm, initiated (in 1882) the successful movement to become a borough in 1890, and was called a Father of Bournemouth in 1902 by the *Graphic*. Not the least of his achievements was the formation of a town fire brigade, including a visit to London with his daughter to choose the first appliance.

In debatable taste, however, Cutler ensured a form of public memorial to himself by installing decorative green and black medallion tiles showing his face at street level; they were in six locations of a terrace of six shops he had completed in Old Christchurch Road, on the south side approaching the Lansdowne. Since this was done in 1877, they have mainly disappeared and one has been chopped in half vertically through the face. Yet the illustration given here is a good likeness which

Joseph Cutler (1830–1910)
An energetic Bournemouth Commissioner is portrayed in a tiled image between shops in Old Christchurch Road. (Author's collection)

has survived remarkably well. However, it failed to impress *The Builder*. In 1883, the magazine expressed the vain hope that 'Bournemouth may rise a little presently to a notion of the desirability of employing a higher class of architecture when any of the streets have to be rebuilt'.

Bibliography

Andrews, Ian and Henson, Frank, *Bournemouth* (The History Press, 2004)

Arnold, Ralph, *The Unhappy Countess* (Constable, 1957)

Ashley, Harry W. and Hugh, *Bournemouth 1890-1990* (Bournemouth Borough Council, 1990)

Bournemouth Borough Council, *Hotel in the Glen: A History of the Town Hall (1881-1985)* (Bournemouth Borough Council, 1986)

Bournemouth Borough Council, *Mayors of Bournemouth 1890-2000* (Bournemouth Borough Council, 2000)

Bradbury, David, *Bournemouth: A Victorian Album* (Past Presented, 2002)

British Medical Association, *Book of Bournemouth* (British Medical Association, 1934)

Bruce, George, *A Fortune and a Family* (Laverstock Books, 1987)

Cave, Paul, *Bournemouth: The Fascinating Story* (Paul Cave Publications Ltd, 1986)

Chilver, Kathleen M., *Holdenhurst, Mother of Bournemouth* (K.M. Chilver, 1956)

Clark, Cumberland, *Life and Works of Cumberland Clark* (Wilding & Son Ltd, 1940)

Cochrane, C., *Poole Bay and Purbeck (2) 1660-1920* (Longmans, 1971)

Cox, Steve, *Urban Trees: A Practical Management Guide* (Crowood Press, 2011)

Dale, R., *Reminiscences of Stourfield* (Dorset County Council, 1975)

Dawson, Leslie, *Wings Over Dorset: Aviation's Story in the South* (Dorset Publishing Co., 1983)

Day Collection of early Bournemouth photographs held at Bournemouth Central Library

Edgington, M.A. *Bournemouth and the First World War* (Bournemouth Local Studies Publications, 1990)

Edwards, Elizabeth, *Famous Folk of Bournemouth, Poole and the Surrounding Area* (Natula Publications, 2006)

_____, *A History of Bournemouth* (Phillimore, 1981)

Gillett, Mildred, *Talbot Village: A Unique Village in Dorset 1850-1989* (Bournemouth Local Studies Publications, 1989)

Granville, A.B., *Spas of England and Principal Sea Bathing Places 2: The Midlands and South* (Adams and Dart, 1841)

Hatts, Leigh, *Bournemouth's Who Was Who* (Natula Publications, 2010)

Hoodless, W.A., *Christchurch Curiosities* (The History Press, 2010)

_____, *Hengistbury Head: The Whole Story* (Poole Historical Trust, 2005)

Hughes, Ted, *Bournemouth Firemen at War* (Wincanton Press, 1991)

Leachman, Revd E.W., *S. Peter's Bournemouth* (Sydenham & Co., 1915)

Leete, Peter B., *Bournemouth and Boscombe Through a New Lens* (Peter B. Leete, 1994)

Legg, Rodney, *Bournemouth Then Meets Now* (Halsgrove, 2009)

Mabey, William, *Bournemouth in 1868* (Bournemouth Local Studies Publications, 1980)

McQueen, Ian, *Bournemouth St Peter's* (Dorset Publishing Co., 1971)

Marshall, Pascoe, *My Story: Memories of Bournemouth and District* (D. Marshall, 1981)

Mate, C.H. and Riddle, C., *Bournemouth 1810-1910* (W. Mate & Sons Ltd, 1910)

Miller, A.J., *Bourne Tregonwell Estate* (A.J. Miller, 1994)

Moore, Wendy, *Wedlock* (Phoenix, 2009)

Norman, Andrew, *Bournemouth's Founders and Famous Visitors* (The History Press, 2010)

Parsons, J.F., *J.E. Beale and the Growth of Bournemouth, Part 3* (Bournemouth Local Studies Publications, 1982)

Peters, John, *Bournemouth Then & Now* (Blandford Press, 1978)

Popham, David, *Bournemouth in 1890* (Bournemouth Local Studies Publications, 1990)

Popham, David and Rita, *The Book of Bournemouth* (Barracuda Books Ltd, 1985)

Rawlings, Keith, *Just Bournemouth* (Dovecote Press, 2005)

Sheppard, Rebecca and Bournemouth University, *Queen's Park in the Liberty of Westover and an Oral History* (Queen's Park Improvement and Protection Society, 2006)

Sherry, Desmond, *Bournemouth: Study of a Holiday Town* (Bournemouth Local Studies Publications, 1978)

Sydenham, J., *The Visitor's Guide to Bournemouth and its Neighbourhood* (J. Sydenham, 1840)

Walker, John, *Bournemouth 1810-2010* (John Walker, 2009)

_____, *St Peter's Church Bournemouth, Notable Personal Memorials* (John Walker, 2004)

West Howe Writers' Group, *West Howe Too! A Changing Corner of Dorset told by Local People Book 2* (Word and Action [Dorset] Ltd Publications, 1983)

Wills, E.G., *Pokesdown and Neighbourhood 1895 to 1910* (Bournemouth Local Studies Publications, 1979)

Young, David S., *The Story of Bournemouth* (Robert Hale, 1957)

Young, J.A., *Bournemouth and the Christchurch Inclosure Act 1802* (Bournemouth Local Studies Publications, 1999)

_____, *Pokesdown and Iford Yesterday* (Bournemouth Local Studies Publications, 2000)

_____, *Pokesdown Past 1750-1900* (Bournemouth Local Studies Publications, 1997)

_____, *Southbourne and Tuckton Yesterday* (Bournemouth Local Studies Publications, 1990)

_____, *Southbourne on Sea 1870-1901* (Bournemouth Local Studies Publications, 1978)

Index

Albany 68
Andromeda 97
Attenuation tank at Bournemouth Pier 95, 96

Balfour case 14
Beale, Nigel 51, 109
Beales
    Father Christmas 49
    fire 109
    package transport 49
    shopwalkers 49
Beckett, Archibald 14
Belle Vue Hotel 29, 83
BIC sculpture 7
Blandford Races 44
Blood Mixture 86
Bonfire Night 1884 105
Boscombe Cottage 19, 27
Boscombe Hippodrome 15
Boscombe Pier 94, 118
Bott, Edmund 39, 55, 57, 59
Bourn House 19, 88, 89, 90
Bourne Belles reclining 45
Bourne Chapel 88, 90
Bourne Chine 8, 25, 28, 38, 40, 44, 46, 83
Bourne Plank 88
Bourne Stream 27, 29, 39, 43, 45, 80, 88, 92, 102, 121
Bourne Tregonwell 7, 28, 29, 30, 39, 82
Bournemouth coat of arms 38
Bournemouth Eye 6, 90
Bournemouth Improvement Act 7, 83
Bournemouth International Centre sculpture 7
Brook, The 81, 88, 89, 90
bucket and spade story 8, 9
Bull, John 103, 104
Burton, Decimus 82, 121
Butterworth, Fred 5, 17

Cedar of Lebanon tree 114
census figures 83, 101
cherry brandy 26
Chine Hotel 5, 17

Christchurch Inclosure Act 79
Christchurch Inclosure Award 20, 27, 37
Churchill, Winston 108
Clark, Cumberland 31
Clark, Sir James 42
Cliff Cottage 11, 19, 44, 45, 47, 80
clock hidden at St Peter's Church 116
Coastal Interceptor Sewer 91–96
Cranborne Road 81
Creeke, Christopher Crabbe 7, 8, 9, 116
Crusoe the Cruiser 14
Cutler, Joseph 121, 122

Dale, Farmer 42
Davies, Trehawke 107
deckchair, world's largest 2
Decoy Cottage 88, 90
Devil statue 14–16
diddycoys 27
Doe, John 23
Doland, Michael 35
Dorset Volunteer Rangers 8, 25, 28, 44
drainage system 91
Drax Grosvenors 25, 44, 47, 80

Ensbury Manor 20, 27, 112

Father Christmas 49
Ferrey, Benjamin 82, 83
fireman's pole 73
Fisherman's Walk 92–92, 101

ghostly horseman 119
ghosts 18, 56, 75, 112, 114
Godfrey, Dan 103
Governor, the 44–47
Grand Theatre and Pavilion 14
Granville, Dr A.B. 39, 82
Gray, George 56
Gulliver, Isaac 20, 27

hair remedy 85, 86
Hamel, Gustav 106

Hard Times 103, 104
Henry VIII 27
Hitchell, J. 52
house on cliff edge 13

Iford House 19, 27
Invalids' Walk 33, 43, ,84, 121

James I 19
Joy, Henry 102, 103

Kinson Manor Farmhouse 20

Labrador 22
Laurel and Hardy 14
leasehold enfranchisement 68, 71, 72
Littledown House 19, 27, 116, 117

Mansion, the 19–21, 24, 28, 29, 39, 44, 45, 47, 48
Manuel, Joseph 89
map of Bourne 1790 89
map of Bourne 1835 80
map of Bourne 1851 81
Marine Village of Bourne 40
Marshall, William 101
Medlycott, Sir Mervyn 24
Mont Dore Hotel 86, 87
mulberry trees 19

Nabarro, Gerald 77
Napoleon 25, 40
National Sanatorium 84, 85
Nelson, Horatio 28

Ogo-Pogo 32, 33, 35
oldest house 19, 112
Old Fire Station 73, 75
Omo the cat 75
Orchard Street 119
ossification 48

Peep into Futurity, A 44, 47
Pelhams House 20, 27
Perseus 97
piano on Boscombe Pier 118
pine trees 32, 33, 37, 79, 85
Pine Walk 43, 84
Portman Lodge 25, 26, 29, 30, 102
Prince Regent 26
Pugs Hole 40, 41

Ranger's Cottage, Hengistbury 19
Rawlings, Keith 8
Red Arrows 62
remedies at watering place 85
Royal Bath Hotel 94

Royal Exeter Hotel 7, 19, 29
Rustic Bridge 89, 102, 103

St Peter's Church 5, 24, 29, 30, 102, 111, 116
Sandymount 10, 12, 13
Sells, Jonathan 7, 8
Shack, The, Throop 21
Shakespeare 21, 32, 34
Shelley Theatre 120
Shettle, Thomas 102
shopwalkers 49
Smith, Mrs Julia 24
smuggling 8, 25, 46, 48, 88, 101, 112
Solent Road 11, 100
Southbourne Cliff Drive 11
Southbourne Coast Road 11, 13
Southbourne Crossroads 10
Southbourne Overcliff Drive 10
spontaneous human combustion (SHC) 53
squirrels 8
Stoney, Andrew Robinson 56, 57, 59, 60
Stourfield House 19, 27, 39, 55–60
Strathmore, Countess of 55, 56, 60
Suchomlin, John 63–67
Sydenham, St Barbe 25, 26, 60
Symes' Cottage 25, 26, 28, 29

Talbot, Georgina 119
Tapps Arms 19, 29, 39
Tapps-Gervis, Sir George 29, 30, 82, 88
Tapps, Sir George Ivison 28, 29, 39, 41, 55, 68, 81
Terrace Cottage 29, 119
Tregonwell Arms 29
Tregonwell, Grosvenor 28, 30
Tregonwell, Henrietta 7, 24, 25, 28–30, 38, 40, 46,
    81, 83
Tregonwell, John 24, 30, 46, 48
Tregonwell, Katherine 25
Tregonwell, Lewis 7, 24–26, 28–30, 32, 38, 40,
    44–46, 48, 55, 60, 79, 81
Tregonwell monument 30
Tregonwell vault 24, 30
Turbary Common 22
turbary 27, 28, 79

Undercliff Drive 61, 97–100
Undercliff Drive monster 97–100

Victoria Cross 8

water tower 121
West, William 27
Westover Road 29, 33, 39, 82, 83, 88, 102, 103
Wreck Ashore, The 120
Whitelegg, Philip 76–78
world record 106–108

First municipal beach hut in the UK
Constructed in 1909, this beach hut on Bournemouth seafront was designed and built by the town's Chief Assistant Borough Engineer and Surveyor, Frederick Percy Dolamore (1869-1951). This 7ft by 7ft hut was the country's first successor to the wheeled Victorian bathing machine. (Courtesy of Matilda Richards)

If you enjoyed this book, you may also be interested in …

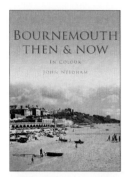

Bournemouth Then & Now

JOHN NEEDHAM

Beautiful archive images are skilfully contrasted with modern photographs taken from the same vantage point today to show how Bournemouth has changed over the last century - as well as the familiar landmarks that have remained. From the gardens as they originally appeared, to the East Cliff Lift, the Cloisters, the model boats once sailed at Children's Corner and the peaceful surroundings of the 'Invalids' Walk', *Bournemouth Then & Now* will delight residents and visitors alike.

978 0 7524 6792 4

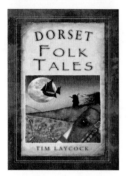

Dorset Folk Tales

TIM LAYCOCK

These lively and entertaining folk tales from one of Britain's most ancient counties are vividly retold by local storyteller Tim Laycock. Their origins lost in the oral tradition, these thirty stories from Dorset reflect the wisdom (and eccentricities) of the county and its people. Dorset has a rich and diverse collection of tales, from the stories of some of Britain's most famous mythical heroes, to tales of demons, dragons, boggarts and sniddlebogs. These stories, illustrated with twenty-five line drawings, bring alive the landscape of the county's rolling hills and Jurassic coast.

978 0 7524 6636 1

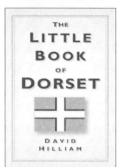

The Little Book of Dorset

DAVID HILLIAM

The Little Book of Dorset is a funny, fast-paced, fact-packed compendium of the places, people, legends and true stories about the county's past and present. Here you can read about Dorset's extraordinary characters, ghostly happenings, royal connections, peculiar traditions, weird pastimes, and curious burials. Not forgotten are the secrets of the fossil-rich coast, towns and villages with odd names and strong literary connections. This is a remarkably engaging little book - essential reading for visitors and locals alike.

978 0 7524 5704 8

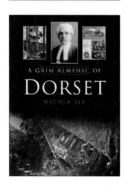

A Grim Almanac of Dorset

NICOLA SLY

This day-by-day catalogue of 365 grim tales from around the county includes tales of highwaymen, murderers, bodysnatchers, duellists, poachers, rioters and rebels. Joining them are accounts of tragic accidents and bizarre deaths, including the soldier who dozed off while smoking on top of the Nothe Fort in 1877 and fell off the parapet. All these, plus tales of fires, shipwrecks, explosions, and accidents by land, sea and air, are here. Generously illustrated, this chronicle is an entertaining and readable record of Dorset's grim past. Read on …if you dare!

978 0 7524 5884 7

Visit our website and discover thousands of other History Press books.

www.thehistorypress.co.uk